STEVESTON

Cannery Row: An Illustrated History

BY
MITSUO YESAKI
AND
HAROLD AND KATHY STEVES

Revised Second Edition

Library and Archives Canada Cataloguing in Publication

Yesaki, Mitsuo, 1936-
Steveston Cannery Row : an illustrated history / by Mitsuo Yesaki and Harold and Kathy Steves. — 2nd ed.

Includes bibliographical references and index.
ISBN 0-9683807-1-9

1. Cannery Row (Steveston, B.C.)—History. 2. Steveston (B.C.)—History. 3. Fishery processing industries—British Columbia—Steveston—History. I. Steves, Harold, 1937- II. Steves, Kathy, 1940- III. Title.

FC3849.S74Y48 2005 971.1'33 C2005-903069-0

Published by Peninsula Publishing Company,
www.peninsulapublishing.ca

Cover Photo:
Sailing vessels tied outside the protection boom off Britannia Cannery with Fraser River skiffs fishing in the background. (ca. 1890)(CRA)

STEVESTON

Cannery Row:

An Illustrated History

Acknowledgements

The authors' most heartfelt gratitude goes to all the people who recounted their experiences and shared their photographic collections. Our thanks to Hisao Atagi, Mick Burdett, Tony Capadouca, Bill Ezaki, Bob Gordon, Haruo Hirata, Bob Karliner, Henry Kokubo, Martin Kuramoto, Kunji and Miyako Kuramoto, Milton Lam, Hideo and Eiji Maeda, Sherman McDonald, Minoru Matsuo, Gerry Miller, Yutaka Mizuguchi, Lloyd Nakade, Tsunezo Nishi, Bobby Nishi, Frank Ross, Yonni Sakai, Paul Sigurgeirson, Bob Stoltz, Arizo Tasaka, Eldon and Rick Thompson, Harry Thompson, Cedric Towers, Joji Yamanaka and Chiyo Yasui.

Jim Woodey and Douglas Stelter provided statistics of Fraser River sockeye and pink salmon landings on file at the Pacific Salmon Commission. The British Columbia Salmon Farmers Association provided recent production figures of farmed salmon from British Columbia and other countries.

Iwakazu Yamamoto and Jerry Takahashi translated relevant sections of various Japanese books. Marilyn Clayton, Mary Gazetas and Shawn Yesaki read the script and suggested appropriate changes and additions.

The maps are based on fire insurance maps of the Steveston waterfront for 1895, 1897, 1911, 1923 and 1946, on file in the Special Collections Division of the University of British Columbia, and detailed maps of the Steveston waterfront for 1936 and 1970 from the Engineering and Planning Departments of the City of Richmond (CR after map). The British Library granted permission to copy plans of the Steveston waterfront from fire insurance maps for 1895, 1897 and 1911 (BL after map). The Insurers Advisory Organization also gave permission to copy plans of buildings from the 1923 and 1946 fire insurance maps (IAO after map).

The majority of the photographs were obtained from the following sources:

City of Richmond Archives	CRA
City of Vancouver Archives	CVA
Delta Museum and Archives	DMA
Harold Steves collection	HS
Irving House Historic Centre Museum	IHHCM
Japanese Canadian National Museum	JCNM
Mitsuo Yesaki collection	MY
New Westminster Public Library	NWPL
University of British Columbia-Special Collections	UBC-SC
Vancouver Maritime Museum	VMM
Vancouver Public Library	VPL

Our apologies to any contributor we may have not acknowledged in this list.

Chinese slitters at butchering table (ca. 1900)(DMA)

Prologue

Steveston is on the southwest corner of Lulu Island at the mouth of the Fraser River. The first settlers on the island were farmers attracted by the fertile soil and flat, treeless land. The prolific runs of sockeye salmon on the Fraser River soon caught the attention of enterprising businessmen hoping to make a fortune on the riches of the sea.

This history attempts to describe and explain the subsequent changes in Steveston's cannery row with its canneries, boat works and fishing craft over the years. It also tells about the living conditions of Native, Chinese, Japanese and Caucasian workers, their homes, schools and health facilities.

Steveston grew from a fishing camp in the late 1870s to the largest fishing town on the British Columbia coast with the largest cannery in the British Empire. Fifteen operating canneries on the waterfront produced 375,000 cases of canned salmon in 1901, and fast clipper ships visited from around the world. Steveston was indeed "the salmon capital of the world".

In "From the Great Lakes to the Wide West" B. McEvoy recalled his visit to the town during the height of the 1901 salmon season. Numerous sailing skiffs waited beside the cannery to unload salmon. Fishermen were paid 12.5 cents per fish. One fisherman gave the landlord of a local hotel $250 for safekeeping, his earnings for the previous week. In the cannery 10,000 to 15,000 fish were stored for processing in a pile 40 feet long by 10 feet wide. Often the canneries could not process such a huge catch, and large quantities of salmon were thrown back into the river.

After a visit in 1910 J. B. Cowen called Steveston "The Queerest Town in Canada" in a magazine article. He described the canneries and fishermen's shacks as derelicts and driftwood washed up from the Gulf of Georgia, and made similar derogatory comments about the inhabitants. The most prominent were Japanese fishermen and Chinese cannery workers. There were lesser

English's (Phoenix) Cannery with Fraser River skiffs and the 'post office' building on the extreme left. (ca. 1890)(VPL)

numbers of Natives and Caucasians, many of whom were fishermen. According to Cowen, fishermen commonly earned from $500 to $1,000 during the short fishing season. Approximately $2,000,000 was invested in the forty canneries and boats on the Fraser River. Six thousand people were employed in this fishery, requiring an estimated $3,200,000 in working capital for wages and costs of materials during a six to seven week period.

Another article by an anonymous author in 1911 described "A Cannery Town in Winter". Steveston was unlike any other fishing town on the coast with its large population of Japanese and Chinese. Japanese boat builders were using tools similar to those used one hundred years earlier to build junks in Japan. This author thought that Steveston had a character that should attract tourists all year round.

Sam Frost in "Steveston's School for Japanese is Busy Place", published in 1936, told how the Japanese contributed to the construction of the Lord Byng School and to the operating costs for after-school classes. Japanese children attended this school for regular classes and an additional hour of Japanese language instruction after 3:00 pm.

In an article "Fishy Business" published in 1937, P .W. Luce warned of the danger to the fishing industry from exploratory salmon fishing by a Japanese research vessel. The ***HAKUYO MARU*** was a 10,000 ton vessel equipped for small scale commercial fish processing. Its small catcher boats gillnetted on the fishing grounds, and the ***MARU*** canned fish and produced fish meal and salt fish. Luce observed that Steveston residents were primarily Japanese, with few Caucasians. There were 400 licensed Japanese fishermen on the Fraser River. The sockeye salmon run of 1936 was better than usual and with the price at 55 cents per fish, many fishermen made more money in a week than most men made in a year. One fisherman caught 7,000 fish which earned him $3,850. Many others made between $1,500 and $2,000 during the big week and considerably more before the run was over.

A very different perspective of the fishing industry was given in a poem found among the Steves' family papers. It was probably written about 1900, when Fraser River fishermen went to sea in sloops and sailing skiffs rigged with sprit sails. These rarely expressed sentiments are universal among women whose husbands and lovers work at sea.

The Scottish Canadian Cannery. (ca. 1905)(HS)

When the Boats Come Home

There is light upon the sea today
And gladness on the strand.
Ah, well you know that hearts are gay
When sails draw nigh the land.
We followed them with thoughts and tears
Far, far across the foam.
Oh, Lord, it seems a thousand years
Until the boats come home.

We tend the children, live our life
And toil and mend the nets,
But is there ever maid or wife
Whose faithful heart forgets?
We know what cruel dangers lie
Beneath the shining foam,
And watch the changes in the sky
Until the boats come home.

There's glory on the seas today;
The sun sets gold and bright,
And the little boats with their silver sails
Sail on through the dusky light.
O'er waves of crystal touched with fire
And flakes of pearly foam,
We gaze to see our heart's desire-
The boats are coming home.

Fishermen in Columbia River type boats. (ca. 1900)(HS)

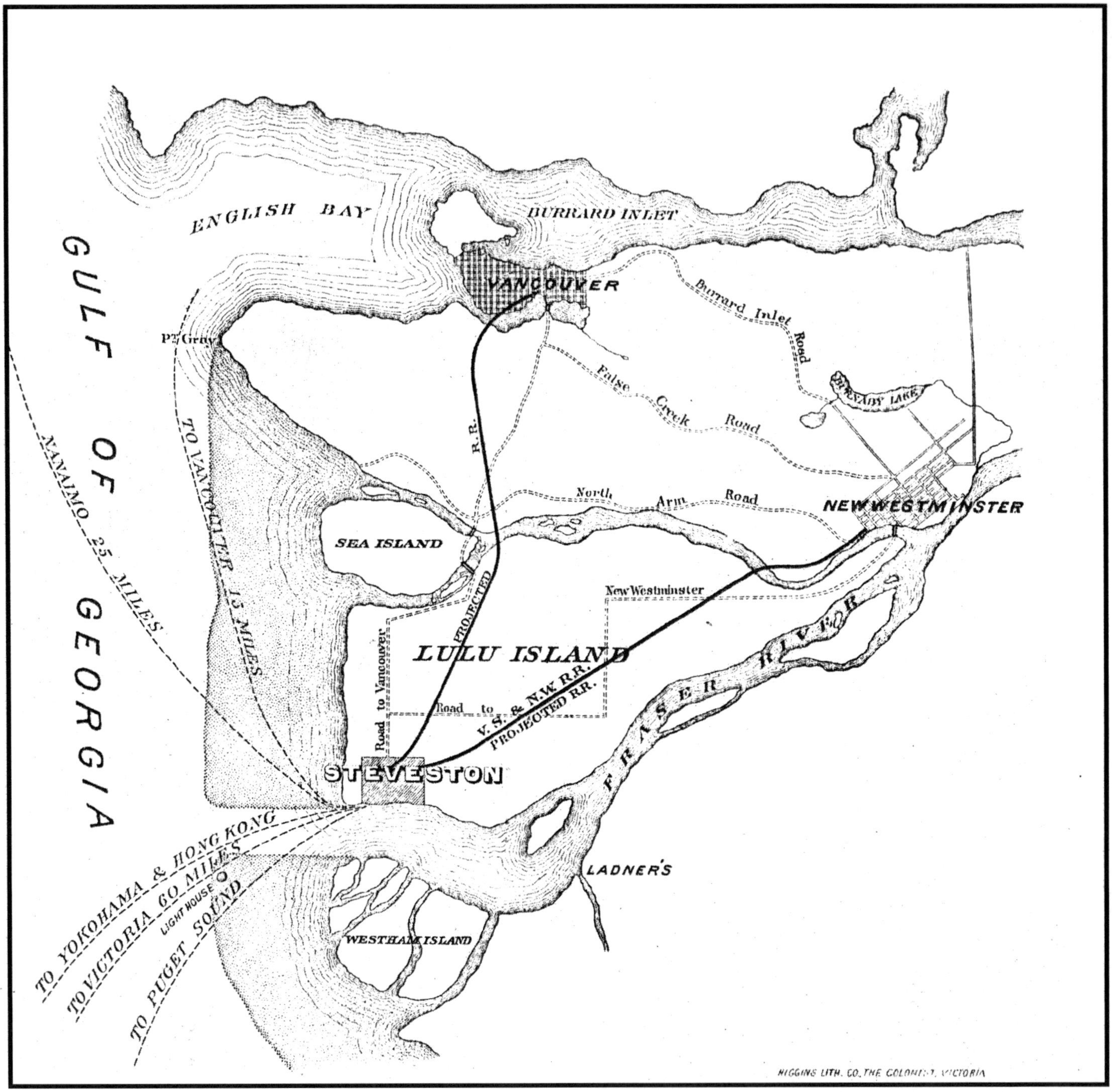

Map of Lulu Island included in W.H. Steves' 1889 pamphlet promoting his land development plan for Steveston. (HS)

The Years of Discovery

Chapter 1

BEFORE 1880

Main Channel of the Fraser River

Lulu, Sea and Westham Islands separate the Fraser River into four channels, called the North Arm, the Middle Arm, the much larger South Arm and Canoe Pass. Before settlers came, numerous sloughs emptied into these channels, supporting runs of coho, pink and chum salmon.

In 1827, the Hudson's Bay Company decided to establish a new trading post called Fort Langley on the lower Fraser River. Captain Aemilius Simpson, commander of the company schooner ***CADBORO***, was ordered to transport supplies for the construction of the post. As there were no charts of the river, Simpson sounded the main channel from Sand Heads to the Fort Langley site. His map shows the North Channel and South Channel, now called Canoe Pass. The channel surveyed by Simpson was probably the Black Buoy Channel as North Sand Heads appears as part of Sturgeon Bank and South Sand Heads as part of Roberts Bank.

Gold miners converged up the Fraser River after the discovery of gold in 1858. Sudden changes in the channel made navigation hazardous, and in May 1859 petitioners demanded the colony anchor a lightship at the Fraser River mouth. The colony purchased a vessel, named her the ***SOUTH SAND HEADS*** and anchored her at the river's mouth, probably on Roberts Bank.

In 1879 this lightship was replaced by the North Sand Heads lighthouse. The lighthouse was an ornate hexagonal wooden tower supported on six iron piles imbedded deep into the sand and braced with stringers. The name suggests the lighthouse stood on North Sand Heads of Sturgeon Bank. The fixed white beacon, fifty-two feet above the seabed, was visible for 12 miles on a clear day. On foggy days, the lighthouse keepers wound the outside bell to peal out a warning every 20 seconds.

Southwest Corner of Lulu Island

Before 1880 a crab apple ridge containing wild Pacific crab apple trees, wild roses, bitter cherry and Indian plum formed a natural sea berm across the west end of Lulu Island. A tall spruce tree at Garry Point on the southwest corner of the island served as a landmark for seafarers. For two miles east of Garry Point the south side of Lulu Island was mainly low, flat treeless prairie except for one patch of spruce trees. Further east, about a quarter of a mile inland, a mixed forest of spruce, cedar, hemlock, alder and yew, bordered by cottonwood, crab apple and elderberry, covered the upstream half of the island except for a central peat bog of shore pine.

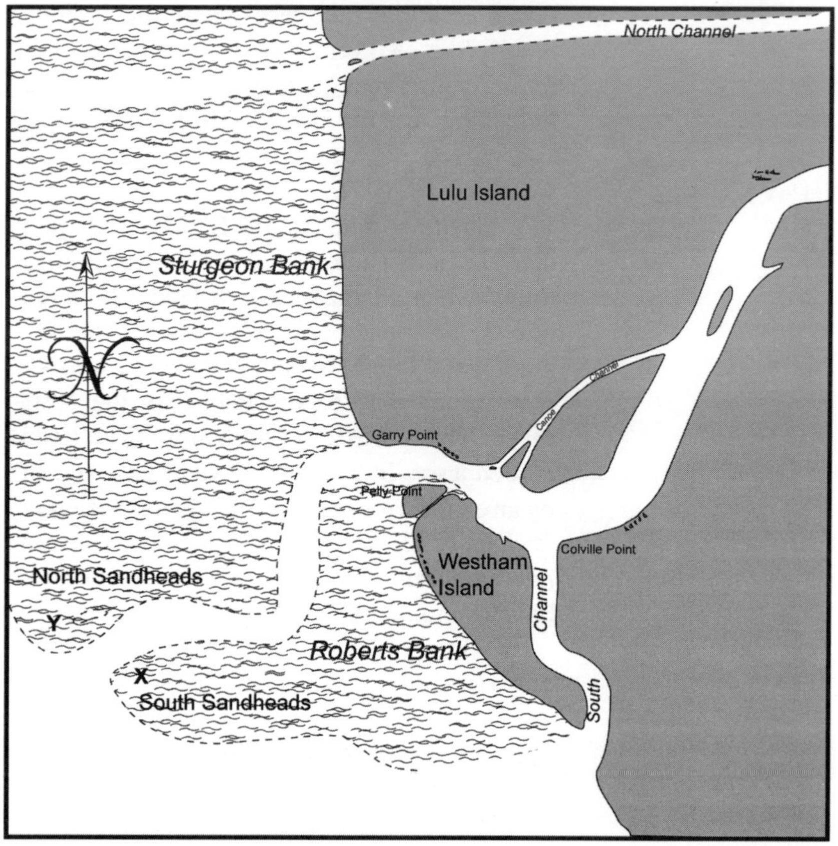

Map of the mouth of the Fraser River surveyed by Aemilius Simpson in 1827. X marks estimated position of the ***SOUTH SAND HEADS*** *Lightship and Y marks estimated position of the North Sand Heads lighthouse. (Copied from London, Hydrographic Office, 1849, Chart 1922)*

Native Settlements

There were two Native settlements at the southwest corner of Lulu Island. "Kwayo7xw" (KWAY-ah-wh), meaning "bubbling water", was a village located at the end of the crab apple ridge at Garry Point. "Kwlhayam" (Kwi-THAY-um), meaning "place having driftwood logs on the beach", was located at the mouth of the "Little Slough" in the vicinity of the

Imperial Cannery. An 1885 chart showed a steep clay bank there, and 1893 maps placed the mouth of the little slough between the Brunswick and Imperial Canneries.

Ida Steves, who arrived in 1878, recalled Garry Point as "the place where the Indians lived". She also remembered that the Steves family sometimes tied up their boat "at the Indian Ranch at the mouth of the Little Slough" and moved it up the slough during stormy weather.

Ida Steves said that the Indians told them that "the Indian houses broke away from Garry Point" when a large chunk of land had fallen into the river and been swept away. An 1871 map of the Imperial Cannery site showed 48 more acres of foreshore land than the 1893 maps. This foreshore land may have been eroded away by a changing river channel, or by an earthquake registering 7.4 on the Richter Scale in 1872. While the exact village locations have not been found, a few Native artefacts have been unearthed along the river shore.

The Natives built wood houses by covering pole frames with cedar planks on mainland sites. These houses were frequently built in long rows to accommodate extended families, but sometimes as single buildings. The Natives also covered pole lean-to frames with woven bulrush mats. They used these mat shelters on short excursions for sturgeon and eulachon in spring, sockeye salmon and berries in summer and coho and chum salmon and bulrushes in fall. In spring the men also hunted deer and beaver, as well as the large herds of seals and sea lions attracted to the eulachon runs.

An old Native couple in front of their summer bulrush mat shelter. (ca. 1900)(HS)

While the Native men were catching fish and hunting game, the women cleaned, dried, smoked and stored the fish. They rendered eulachons into oil, a staple in their diet, and continually checked the stored fish to prevent spoilage. The Native women and children dug clams and cockles, gathered salmonberries and gooseberries, and dug young horsetail shoots and roots of silverweed and clover.

Native Fishing

For sturgeon fishing in winter, the Native men crewed a canoe about twenty feet long. One man probed the river bottom with a forked harpoon on a pole up to fifty feet long. When he located a fish, he quickly plunged the harpoon points, with a strong cord attached, into the sturgeon. A sturgeon could be ten feet long and weigh over 600 pounds. A large sturgeon would drag the canoe behind it at a rapid pace. Sometimes the men used a heavy stone on a cedar bark rope as an anchor to help slow the canoe down. When the fish eventually tired, they brought it close to the canoe, and struck it on the head. The fish dove, the first man slowly retrieved it on the line, and another man dealt another blow. This continued until the completely exhausted fish lay beside the canoe. They leaned over until the gunwale was at the water level, and flipped the fish into the canoe. Then they stepped back to right the canoe. Before the sturgeon began to thrash about, one man stabbed a sharp knife into the nape of its head to sever the spinal cord. They brought the fish to land, cut it up and distributed part among the tribe to be eaten fresh. Then they smoked and stored the rest of the fish. In summer sturgeon could be caught in sloughs with nets and weirs and shorter harpoons usually used for spearing seals.

The Natives fished for eulachons with dipnets, bagnets and herring rakes. A herring rake was a narrow cedar pole about ten feet long, flattened to make one end about two inches wide and a half inch thick. Originally, it was fitted along one edge with sharp teeth made from bone splinters. Later nails were driven with their heads filed to sharp points. One Native stood or knelt near the bow with the rake, and another sat at the stern, paddling to keep the canoe on a steady course. The fisherman swished the rake up through the water, and shook the impaled fish into the canoe behind him with a sharp knock on the gunwale.

The Natives also used weirs and traps to harvest salmon from the summer freshet until late autumn. They built weirs along the riverbanks of main channels and across many sloughs on the island. To build the weirs they drove pilings into the riverbed at regular intervals and lashed latticeworks of branches to the pilings. These weirs were especially effective in diverting coho, pink and chum salmon into latticework traps, where the men impaled the salmon with spears and gaffs.

In the fall more Coast Salish Natives arrived to catch, smoke and dry pink and chum salmon, their principal winter food. At the end of November they loaded their dugout canoes, and returned to their winter residences.

The First Caucasian Settlers

Around 1860 Lulu Island was surveyed by the Corps of Royal Engineers into 160-acre lots called quarter sections. Many of the sections on the western part of the island were sold by the time Manoah Steves arrived at the island in 1877. He liked the rich delta soil and tidal flats so similar to his former farm in Coverdale, New Brunswick, and wrote back to his family in Maryland to follow him out to the west coast. He purchased 400 acres north of what is now Steveston Highway for about 75 cents an acre from Edward A. Sharpe. Part of this land was under water at high tide, so Steves went to Victoria and bought an additional 300 acres of higher, drier land.

The Steves family, consisting of Martha and her six children, William Herbert, Josephine, Joseph, Mary Alice, Ida and Walter, arrived at their new home aboard the side-wheel steamer ***ENTERPRISE*** on the morning of May 24, 1878. The captain was astonished when the family wanted to land at Garry Point, as no one lived there except an old bachelor named Sharpe. He advised them to continue on to New Westminster, or at least to Ladner's Landing. However, Martha Steves could not be deterred, so the captain stopped the vessel in mid-stream, and the family and their possessions were ferried ashore in a rowboat. Manoah Steves and Edward Sharpe were waiting for them on a huge log on the riverbank. After a joyous reunion, they picked up their luggage, and trudged three-quarters of a mile inland along wild cattle trails to Sharpe's shack between present day Sixth and Seventh Avenues just south of Steveston Highway. Sharpe kindly let the family live in his shack until they were able to build their own home. The shack was very small, about 12 feet by 12 feet. Martha, young Walter and the three girls slept in the shack, while Sharpe, Manoah and the two older boys slept in the barn.

Joseph Steves beside the original Steves' residence built in 1878. A bedroom on the right was added at a later date. The house was originally on six-foot piles until the dyke was built after the 1905 flood. (ca. 1910)(HS)

The new Steves' home was built west of present day Seventh Avenue and north of Steveston Highway. It was a two-story building, 12 feet by 20 feet with a large living room/kitchen downstairs and two bedrooms upstairs for the six children. The house was heated by a wood stove with a stovepipe instead of a chimney. The door was made of boards nailed together like a barn door, but the windows had real glass panes brought in by steamboat. The house was built on six-foot piles to escape the high tides of May and June that flooded the west end of the island. An earthen dike was built around the backyard. In the next few years, the house was enlarged by adding a kitchen on the south side of the building and a long, narrow bedroom on the east.

There was abundant game, fish and fruit. Ducks and geese were so plentiful that Manoah shot as many as 150 birds at a time with his eight-gauge shotgun. Instead of plucking feathers off the birds, the girls cut off the heads and wings, peeled off the skin and salted down the carcasses for future use. Manoah knotted his own net to catch salmon for eating fresh and salting for winter use. The boys dug clams and cockles on the tidal flats. They also dip-netted eulachons and bought eulachons and sturgeon from the Natives. The girls gathered crab apples, salmonberries and gooseberries for making jams and preserves.

Obtaining drinkable water was one of the biggest problems for the new settlers. The clay soil made wells impractical. Water from tidal pools was clean enough for washing dishes, clothes and floors, but not for drinking. Rain was collected in barrels to drink, but was always infested with wiggling insects. If there was no rain, the men would row out to the middle of the river and collect relatively clean water from the remnants of fresh mountain streams.

Manoah, Herbert and Joseph cleared a small patch of land and borrowed Sharpe's team of oxen, as the ground was too wet to plow with a horse, to plant oats and hardy vegetables. They stored potatoes, turnips and cabbages in an above-ground, mud-covered "root cellar" because the ground was too wet for the usual underground pit. The Steves' first calf came from a cow rented from a neighbour, the second was purchased from another settler, and the third just wandered through the fence into their garden one day. The oats were planted late and grew poorly in the salty, wet soil. They were harvested green and used as winter fodder for the three calves.

Thick underbrush, boggy terrain and poor trails made land travel extremely difficult. Early settlers used rowboats for shopping, visiting and attending church and other meetings. Nathan Woodward, one of the early Fraser River fishing boat-builders, built a rowboat for Herbert Steves in exchange for the new breach-loading, double-barrelled shotgun Herbert had brought from Maryland. The nearest store for the Steves family was at New Westminster, 17 miles upriver. There they bought flour, salt, rice, coal oil, candles and soap.

A freighter-type, steam-powered tenderboat used to transport fish from the fishing grounds to the canneries. (ca. 1900)(HS)

The First Fish Camp

Marshall Martin English emigrated from California and built a fish cannery opposite New Westminster at Brownsville in 1877. He established a fish camp at the southwest corner of Lulu Island near the Kwlhayam village, where he bought salmon caught by Native fishermen. Native tribes had been migrating for centuries to the island to harvest salmon. Now the Natives in their traditional dugout canoes fished for English. The fish were transported to his Brownsville cannery by two steam-powered boats. The river freighter ***LEONORA*** carried fish in its hold or in boxes on deck, and the tugboat ***LEVIATHAN*** towed a pot scow full of fish.

Manoah Steves' daughter Josephine wrote in a letter dated November 18, 1878, about a family trip to visit one of their nearest neighbours.

We went over to Mr. Kirkland's a few days ago...across the river, 5 or 6 miles from here. They live on the mainland about half a mile from Mr. Ladner's. We went in a rowboat across the river. We went about a mile in the first hour, had a headwind, then we stopped at a fishing camp, about half an hour, until the steamboat that carried the fish came along. We had our boat fastened to it and we got into the steamboat and went almost there, so we got into our boat and sailed there.

The Steves generally kept their boat by the Indian camp at the foot of the crab apple ridge trail at Garry Point, and the fish camp at the English site was one mile east. While visiting the Kirklands the Steves family probably picked up their mail at Ladner's Landing Post Office.

Chapter 2

The Years of Development

1880 - 1889

Municipality and Waterfront

The Municipality of Richmond, incorporated in 1879, completed Number Two Road across Richmond in 1883. The road was known then as the "Trunk Road" but later as the "Vancouver Road". By 1887 workers had also built Number One Road, Number Three Road, Number Four Road and Number Nine Road (later called Steveston Highway). However, the principal mode of transportation during this decade was by water with rowboats, steam tugs and ferries. Land travel on Lulu Island remained difficult and essentially confined to walking. Residents became known as "mud flatters", and wore gum-boots and carried slippers when they went visiting.

The first two trade licenses issued in 1882 by the Municipality of Richmond were to Marshall English for the Phoenix Cannery and to J.H. Todd and Sons for the Richmond Cannery on Sea Island. In 1882 Marshall English and his partner Samuel B. Martin purchased land from Elzear Gerard, and built the Phoenix Cannery east of their fish camp. Around 1884 English moved his wife and eight children into a house built for them near the Phoenix Cannery. On the wharf in front of the cannery he built a post office.

John Wesley Sexsmith, who was reeve (mayor) of Richmond from 1887 to 1892, was able to use the cannery wharf for his ferry service. In 1882 his steam ferry ***ALICE*** began making daily trips from this site, transporting passengers and light freight to New Westminster, Ladner's Landing and other landings along the way. Mail continued to be addressed to "Ladner's Landing Post Office" and then transferred by ferry to English's post office.

The London brothers, Charles and William, arrived in Richmond from Ontario in 1880, buying 200 acres of land from Thomas McNeely at the south end of Number Two Road. The Lulu Island Post Office was established at London's Landing on September 1, 1884, and continued to operate there until 1924.

After 1884 London's Landing was used by the ferry ***ALICE***, now owned by Captain F. W. Stewart. The side-wheel steamer ***ENTERPRISE*** ran twice a week in the summer and once a week in the winter between London's Landing, Ladner's Landing, New Westminster and Victoria. In 1886 William London opened a general store and temperance hotel (boarding house) near the wharf. In 1887 the ***ALICE*** was replaced by a new boat, which burned soon after. The large London farmhouse was built after Charles London married Henrietta Dalziel in 1888.

First Schools and Churches

In 1884 the empty post office building on the English wharf became the area's first school run by Virginia English and her mother. Virginia taught her three younger brothers as well as Jane and Bob Blair, Mabel Branscombe, Mary London, Walter Steves and other children of early settlers. English also

Map of the Steveston waterfront showing canneries in 1889.

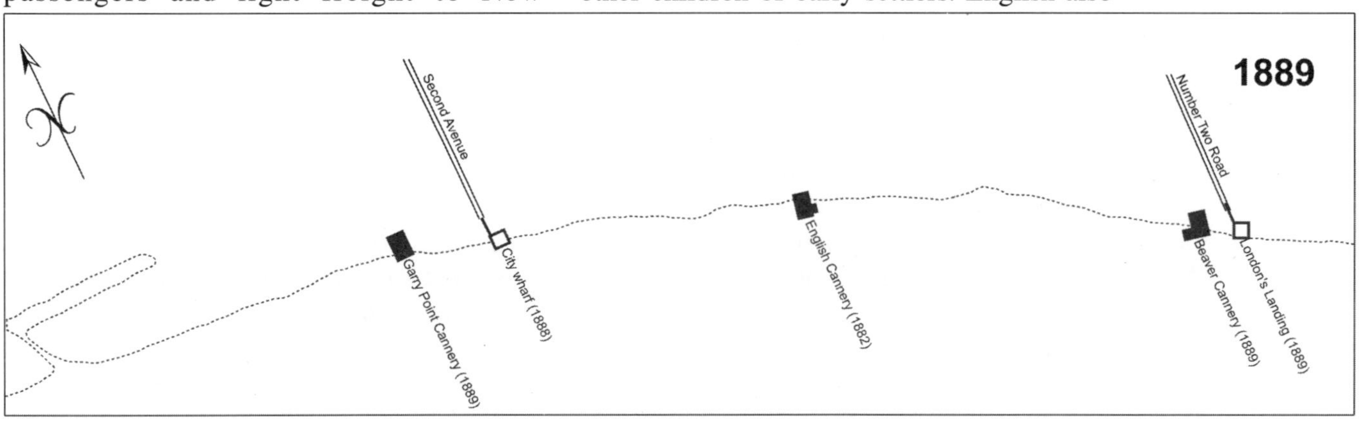

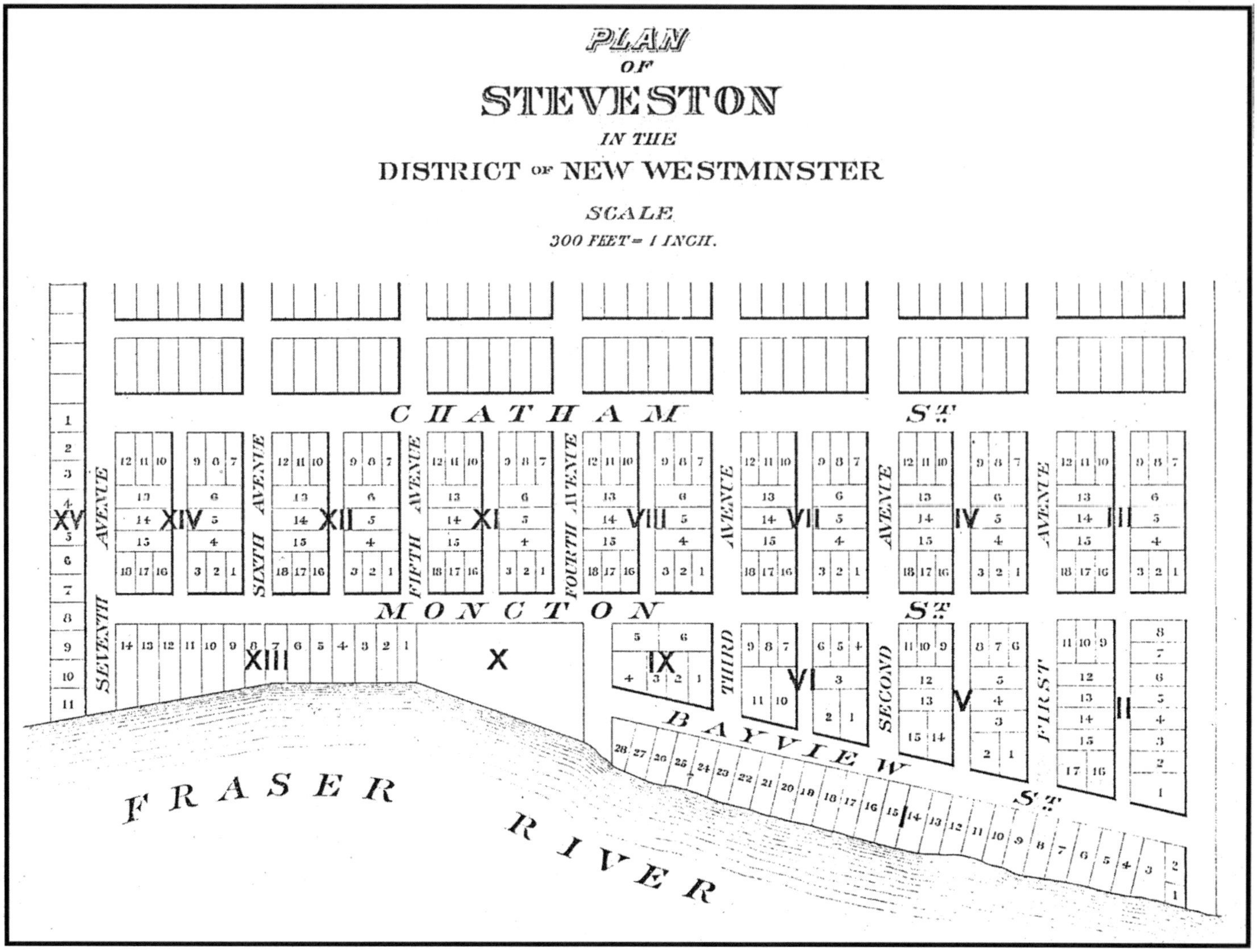

Plan of Steveston included in W.H. Steves' 1889 pamphlet promoting the development of the town site. (HS)

built a Catholic church north of the Phoenix Cannery as his wife was a Catholic. When the English family went to California for a year in early 1887, school classes were transferred to a new church at London's Landing. Mr. Robertson, a retired teacher from Ontario, rowed across the river from Westham Island every day to teach there.

In 1888 the provincial government built Richmond's first school, a little brown one-room building at the corner of Number Two Road and Number Nine Road (Steveston Highway). English School was named after Marshall English, who became one of the first trustees of the English School District. The first teacher there, Mr. Muir, had his teaching certificate taken away when he complained about the curriculum to the newspapers.

Steves' Town Site

Land speculation soared on the west coast with the completion of the Canadian Pacific Railway to Vancouver in November 1885. William Herbert Steves, Manoah's eldest son, was Richmond's first major developer and speculator. It is unclear whether his main motive was to make a profit or to fulfill his vision of a great port at the mouth of the Fraser River. In 1886 he bought 160 acres north of Chatham Street. He then borrowed $41,000 at 12 percent interest to buy the remaining 55 acres of the future Steveston town site from T. S. Bone, and two other large tracts of land in East Richmond from other landowners. His mortgage company was B. C. Land, a consortium of British financiers with their head office in London, England.

On June 19, 1888, he asked the consortium to release four lots along what is now Second Avenue. He was the first seedsman on the west coast, and he used one of the lots to establish his seed store that year. He sold the other three lots to James Crook, James C. Forlong who built the first general store in 1890, and Walter "Billy" Steeves, who later operated a stagecoach to Vancouver. On July 23, 1888, Steves asked the consortium for a further advance of $1,500 to build a wharf at the foot of Second Avenue. On March 5, 1889, he asked for the release of two acres at the foot of Fourth Avenue for sale to Hobson and Company for the construction of the Garry Point Cannery. He spent the down payment for this sale on improvements on the wharf, and built an Opera House and the Richmond Hotel on Second Avenue. The wharf was called Steves' Landing or City Wharf.

In 1889 Herbert Steves subdivided his half-mile square townsite into lots 30 foot wide for a town site. He issued a pamphlet with a map to promote his development. The front page of this pamphlet stated: "The Town of STEVESTON has a great future, the deepest water and best harbour on the Fraser River".

Development of the Commercial Fishery

Marshall English built a fish trap near his fish camp. However, the government banned the use of fish traps in the Fraser River, as well as seine nets which encircled the salmon and gillnets which were anchored to pilings. Only gillnets which drifted behind a boat were permitted. There were also limits on the length of nets and the size of mesh in the gillnets, which determined the size of salmon caught. Smaller fish swam right through the mesh. Larger ones could not enter the mesh. Nets had to be kept at least 250 feet apart and could not block more than one-third of the river's width.

The number of licensed fishing units for the Fraser River increased from 285 in 1877 to 935 in 1887, when the dominion government imposed restrictions limiting the number of licenses to 500 for each of the next four years. Each cannery was only allowed twenty licenses.

Fishing was permitted throughout the week, with a short closure on the weekend. The commercial catch of sockeye salmon increased from 0.1 million fish in 1876 to 4.5 million in 1889. Catches of sockeye vary in a four-year cycle, because salmon return upriver to spawn at four years of age. In the 1880s the catches in 1881, 1885 and 1889, the dominant years, averaged 2.2 million fish, while the catches in the off-years averaged 0.8 million (Appendix Table l).

Canneries

The first canneries were built around New Westminster. The fishery expanded rapidly, and soon canneries were sited along all branches of the river. Three canneries were built in the Steveston area in the 1880s, the Phoenix Cannery in 1882, and the Garry Point Cannery and the Beaver Cannery in 1889.

The canneries were built on a foundation of pilings driven into the river bed, extending from the shore to beyond the low water level. Planks were laid over the pilings to provide a large wharf area with ready access to the river. This was the most cost effective way to get a stable foundation for a large and heavy cannery building. The river also provided an easy, cheap means of disposing wastes.

Building materials for early canneries were brought to Steveston from New Westminster by barges. Cannery buildings were built using post and beam construction with either board and batten or horizontal channel siding, all precut at the Brunette Sawmill or the Royal City Planing Mills in New Westminster. For example, on August 27,

From the left, the City Wharf with shed, the Garry Point Cannery in the background, W.H Steves' seed store (dark-coloured building), J.C. Forlong's general store (white building), Kenneth Sweet's butcher shop and O.D. Sweet's real estate office. (1890)(CVA)

English's (Phoenix) Cannery with the 'post office' building on the wharf, moored Native dugout canoes, a houseboat along the river edge and gillnets racked on land. (ca. 1885)(IHHCM)

1889, Manoah Steves ordered "3 lots of cull lumber; 3,500 feet of 1 X 12-inch, 16-foot long; 4 pieces of 4 X 6-inch, 32-foot long; to be delivered to Steveston". Brunette Sawmills sent the order with the following note: "Please unload this scow at once as we require it on Saturday, to load for up river." With the 1 X 12-inch used for board and batten siding, this was enough lumber for a barn or stable, with walls 16 feet high and 60 to 70 feet long and 32 feet wide. Lumber for canneries would have been similarly ordered and delivered to the construction site.

Phoenix Cannery (1882)

Built in 1882, the Phoenix Cannery was generally called English's Cannery while Marshall English owned it. This cannery was a long building sited west of a slough and perpendicular to the bank of the Fraser River. The river end of the structure was one storey and open to facilitate the landing of fish. The land end of the building was two storeys with the canning line on the lower level and storage space and a net room on the upper level. The cannery operated in 1883 and 1884, and every year from 1886 to 1895 when it was destroyed by fire. It was purchased by Anglo British Columbia Packing Company Limited in 1891.

A chief carpenter with a work crew on top of lumber for construction of a cannery building. (ca. 1900)(HS)

Garry Point Cannery (1889)

In 1889 George Hobson persuaded Charles Windsor, a foreman of the Inverness Cannery on the Skeena River, to become his partner. Hobson was to provide the funds and Windsor the expertise for a new cannery. When the Garry Point Cannery was well under construction, and Windsor owed money to all his suppliers, Hobson told him that there were no more funds. They managed to secure a $4,000 loan from Turner-Beeton and Company in Victoria, and continued their venture. They packed 13,716 cases of canned salmon that year, and were able to pay off all their debts. Their manager and foreman was William Rose Lord, whose father had built the first salmon cannery on the Columbia River around 1865. They operated the cannery in 1890, and sold it in 1891 to Anglo British Columbia Packing Company Limited for $35,000.

The map commissioned by W.H. Steves in 1889 subdividing the Steveston site showed the entire waterfront partitioned into small lots, except for the two acre lot at the foot of Fourth Avenue which was shown as Block X. Steves had already sold this lot to George Hobson and Company in April 1889.

(Beaver) Richmond Cannery (1889)

The Beaver Cannery was built at a site west of Number Two Road by Jacob Hunter Todd and Sons in 1889. This was the first L-shaped cannery in the Steveston area. It was renamed the Richmond Cannery in 1905. It operated every year from 1889 until it was destroyed by fire in May 1924. The cannery and facilities for workers and fishermen were never rebuilt.

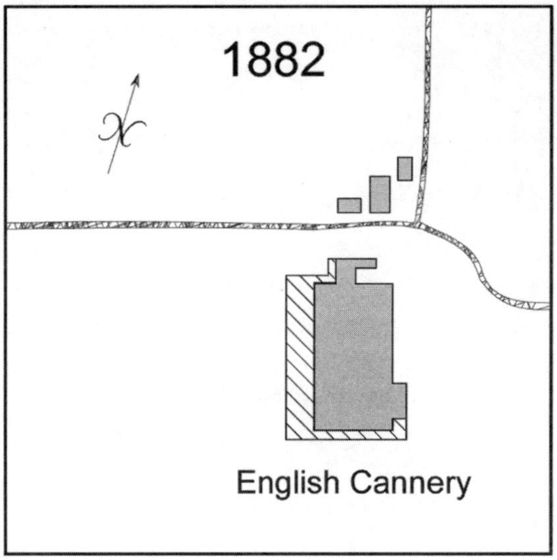

General plan of English's (Phoenix) Cannery. (modified BL)

Making Cans

Each cannery operation on the Fraser River generally commenced in February with the arrival of the Chinese can-making crew. The first task was making solder bars. Pig lead and pig tin were melted in a large cauldron set in a brickwork stove. The molten mixture was ladled out and poured into bar molds. The 15-inch, half-round bars and 12-inch, triangular bars would be used to solder the bottoms and lids on the cans.

Between 300,000 and 1,000,000 cans were required for the salmon season, depending upon the salmon harvest expected. The cans were made from tin sheets imported from Great Britain. Can-making required six separate steps and machines. The can bodies were cut with a square shear, and the bottoms and tops were stamped out from tin sheets with a press. These cutting tools were powered by foot pedals. The can bodies were then passed through a set of rollers in the forming machine to shape them into cylinders.

The cylinders were next slipped onto the seaming machine to solder the seams. This machine had a sloped spool, with the same diameter as the can. Two clamps, controlled by a treadle, held the cylinder firmly on the spool while muriatic acid was applied on the seam with a small brush. A small piece of triangular solder was placed on the seam, and melted and spread with a soldering iron.

Then the bottoms were put on the soldered cylinders. These cylinders with bottoms were passed through the crimping machine. As the horizontal spool on this machine revolved half-a-turn, the flared edge of the bottom was firmly crimped against the can body by the two fixed bars above and below the spool.

The crimped cans were placed in trays of twenty-four and taken to the soldering machine to solder the bottoms to the bodies. The soldering machine consisted of two troughs. The first contained braided cotton lamp wick soaked with acid, and the second had solder kept in the molten state by a coal fire under the trough. The cans were placed on a short, tilted and sloped track. As they rolled down the slope, their bottom edges were painted with the acid from the wick. As each can passed through the acid trough, it came in contact with an endless, moving chain and a long bar. The manually-driven chain rotated the cans, held

Cannery row: from the right, Lulu (London) Cannery under construction, J.C. Forlong's general store (white building between pilings), W.H. Steves' seed store, City Wharf with shed and Garry Point Cannery. (ca. 1890)(CVA)

A large catch of salmon piled on cannery floor, and Chinese slitters butchering fish. (ca 1890)(HS)

in a tilted position by the bar, through the molten solder. From the solder trough, the cans rolled onto a 30-foot sloping track to cool. Three thousand cans could be soldered with this machine in a ten-hour day. At the end of the track the cans were taken to the packing room, and stored upside down in a pile six feet high until the canning season.

Salmon Canning Operations

In its early years the salmon canning industry depended on a large work force. The many steps in the canning process included making cans, gutting and cutting fish, filling cans, soldering lids and vents, testing seals, and varnishing and labelling cans. Everything was done manually by Native women and Chinese men. Each canning line was a row of tanks, tables, and benches equipped with manually driven machines. Wood-fired boilers produced steam to heat the hot water kettles and retorts. The steam was also used to power water pumps for washing fish, and cleaning the premises. Chinese labourers moved fish and materials with baskets, trays and hand trucks. The machines increased the productivity of the canning process from 240 cases per day with a 130-150 man crew in 1877 to 1,000 cases per day with a 120-140 man crew in 1883. Each case contained 48 one-pound cans or 96 half-pound cans.

The canning season started in July with the arrival of the sockeye salmon, the main species canned on the Fraser River before 1900. Fish had to be canned within 48 hours after they were caught. First Chinese slitters cut off the head and fins and slit open the belly. Competent slitters could butcher four to five fish in a minute. Each slitter had from two to five knives which he kept razor sharp at all times. The slitters dropped the dressed fish into tanks of running salt water. Native women slimers took out the guts, scrubbed the body cavity clean and scraped off the remaining scales in the sliming tanks. Then they placed the fish into hoppers to drain.

The drained fish were taken to the hand-operated gang knives, which had eight blades spaced to cut each fish into steaks exactly the length of the can. The steaks were then split by Chinese choppers with 16-inch knives, and the pieces dropped into wooden tubs. When the tubs were full, they were carried by Chinese workers to parallel filling tables and the contents dumped into a raised V-groove in the centre of each table.

The cans were arranged in trays and, before being filled with fish, were seeded with a little salt from a salting board. This device covered two trays of cans and consisted of a top board and a bottom sliding board, both of which were perforated so that there was a hole over each can. The holes of the top board were closed when the bottom board was pulled out. Salt was placed in the holes and the bottom board pushed back to drop the salt into the cans.

The cans were filled with the salmon pieces by two rows of Native women fillers. Each filler had a filling case, which was a small box with an open front and a hinged metal lid. The lid had a round hole with a rim which fit inside the top of the can. This made it easy to fill the can with pieces of salmon without soiling the outer side of the can. An expert filler could fill twelve cans in four minutes.

Then the trays of filled cans were hand-trucked to the wipers' tables. Chinese wipers cleaned the cans with old gillnet webbing and then passed them across the table to the cappers. A Chinese capper placed a piece of tin on the fish and the top onto the can, making sure that the vent hole of the top was over the piece of tin. He tapped the top securely onto the can with a piece of wood and replaced it into the tray. Chinese workers took the trays to the crimping machines to crimp the tops firmly onto the cans. After crimping, the cans rolled to the soldering machines to solder the tops to the cans. Chinese workers picked up the cans as they rolled out of the soldering machine and arranged them in woven iron coolers. The filled coolers were then trucked to Chinese stoppers who soldered shut the vent holes.

The coolers with topped cans were next taken to the bath-room crew for cooking. The Chinese men who made cans in the spring generally were the bath-room crew. They suspended the coolers by block and tackle and lowered them into hot water testing kettles. They looked for air bubbles forced out of leaks from the faulty cans, and soldered the leaks.

The coolers were taken to the cooking tanks for the initial cooking in boiling water heated by steam pipes. After cooking for an hour, the coolers were taken out and placed on hand trucks. Steam in the cans was released by punching a hole in the top with a sharp-pointed mallet. The holes were soldered shut while the cans were still hot. The coolers were then lifted off the trucks and immersed in the hot water kettles to test for leaks. After testing, the coolers were stacked onto trucks on rails leading to the steam retorts for the final cooking. The cans of salmon were cooked in steam maintained at 240 degrees Fahrenheit for one hour. After this cooking, the trucks were wheeled out of the retorts to the hot water kettles where the coolers were immersed again to test the cans for leaks. The coolers with the canned salmon were next washed with hot caustic soda, rinsed with cold water and then loaded onto trucks and taken to the packing

Native women cleaning and washing fish. (ca. 1890)(IHHCM)

The interior of the Phoenix Cannery with Marshall English and a boy on cans of salmon ready for labelling and boxing for export. (ca. 1890)(VPL)

room.

The coolers were spread out in the packing room to allow the cans to cool. A Chinese tester tapped each can with a small hammer-like tool with a ball head. He was able to detect faulty or underweight cans by the sound and rebound of this tool. He set aside the rejects to be redone. Other Chinese workers piled the good cans to a height of 14 to 15 cans. After the cans had cooled thoroughly, the tester tested the cans a second time with the tapping tool. The other workers piled the cans in a nearby area.

A normal working day was ten hours with a half hour off for lunch. If considerable numbers of fish remained after the normal shift, workers came back after a half hour break for supper to process as much of the catch as possible. Occasionally cannery crews worked fifteen to eighteen hour days during the height of the sockeye season.

The Native women were supervised by the Chinese boss. They were identified by numbers stamped on their tin tags. The Caucasian cannery bookkeeper kept records of the hours the women worked and their purchases at the company store.

The canning season was over by about mid-September, and Chinese workers began the task of boxing the canned salmon. They glued labels onto the cans, packed the cans into wooden boxes and nailed on the tops. The boxed canned salmon was then ready for export to world markets.

Cannery Workers

During the 1880s the cannery workers were mainly Native women and Chinese men. Natives from the Musqueam and Tsawwassen villages of the Fraser River delta arrived at the canneries early in the year. Natives from various localities on Vancouver Island and the Gulf Islands and as far away as the Queen Charlotte Islands and the upper reaches of the Skeena and Nass Rivers arrived later. The Natives from the southern coast travelled in two types of canoes, small ones for one or two persons, and large ones for families and household needs. Natives from the northern coast had larger canoes with higher sterns. The canoes were sometimes rigged with sails for easier travel. Canneries competed for the Native women who were the best at making and mending nets and working on the canning lines. Cannery managers who understood Chinook, the trade jargon spoken by Natives,

Natives travelling from their coastal villages in dugout canoes to work for the Fraser River canneries. (ca. 1885) (HS)

were more successful in recruiting these women as net makers and cannery workers and their husbands as fishermen.

The Chinese began arriving in British Columbia in the late 1850s to take part in the Fraser River gold rush. In the 1880s about 17,000 Chinese men were contracted to help build the Canadian Pacific Railway. When the railway was completed in 1885, some returned to China, but many others chose to stay in Canada. To counter the rising resentment of the Caucasian population towards Orientals, the federal government passed the Federal Chinese Immigration Act of Canada in 1885, imposing a tax of $50 on each immigrant from China.

Cannery managers made agreements with Chinese contractors for crews of Chinese workers on a per case production basis. The contract system had many advantages for cannery managers. They were relieved of the hassle of hiring experienced workers for the season. They were able to calculate in advance the precise cost of producing a case of canned salmon. They could provide accommodations with only the basic amenities. A Chinese boss was able to get more work out of contracted workers, than when the same workers were paid a daily salary by the cannery manager. Finally, any losses incurred in hiring the workers were absorbed by the contractor. Some contractors paid the $50 head tax, and the worker had to pay this back out of his wages.

The contractor was paid an advance and the balance on completion of the season's pack. He was responsible for hiring, disciplining, housing and feeding the workers. He charged each worker an employment fee, but his highest profit was gained by inflating the costs of food and other essentials. After deducting his fees and expenses, the contractor divided the remaining amount among the crew. After a poor pack of canned salmon, Chinese workers often had little to show for their labour.

Cannery Houses

Caucasians were employed in the canneries along the Steveston waterfront in supervisory positions as managers, foremen, technicians and bookkeepers. The manager and sometimes the foreman were provided with company houses for their families. Technicians and book keepers were housed in bunk houses on cannery premises.

Natives working at the first canneries lived at their own village sites. Later, the canneries provided the Natives with housing sites called "rancheries". Sometimes temporary canvas tents were pitched near the cannery where the men delivered their catch and the women worked. More permanent wooden structures were built in rows of one-room units like traditional longhouses. The walls and shed roofs were constructed of split cedar boards or sawn board and batten lumber. Earlier structures had no windows, and the doors were sometimes just openings covered with rush mats. They were sometimes built

Tents pitched beside a cannery and used as living quarters by Native families during the salmon canning season. (ca. 1890) (IHHCM)

Native fishermen in Fraser River skiffs delivering fish to the Garry Point Cannery. (ca. 1890)(CVA)

above water on stilts like other cannery buildings. Later structures had doors and windows. Over each door hung a board with the number of the skiff fished by the occupant. If an accident happened on the fishing grounds, relatives could be quickly identified and contacted. The beds were boards on posts against one wall, with rush mats or blankets for bedding. The seats were boxes or boards on the floor.

Some of the rooms had earthen floors. A fire in the centre of the room provided warmth, and was used for cooking whenever food was prepared indoors. A hole in the roof of each room allowed smoke to escape. The Native women cooked meals over open fires, outdoors or indoors. They baked pilot bread of flour and water in an open pan. Their staple foods included salmon, sturgeon, eulachans, clams and cockles. They also ate eulachan oil, currants, wild rhubarb, a kind of greens and various berries.

Many of the huts had smokehouses for curing fish. Each smokehouse consisted of posts with a roof and a rush mat that was moved from side to side to serve as a windbreak. Salmon were beheaded and split in half with their backbones removed. Pieces of wood were inserted to hold the carcasses flat. Then some of the split salmon were hung in rows under the roof and smoked over a slow fire. Others were salted in brine.

Eulachons were smoked on strings hung through their gills and mouths, or rendered into oil for food and for fuel in lamps. Eulachons were also sun-dried on planks or strings. The Natives cured enough salmon and eulachons to tide them over the winter.

The bunkhouses built for the Chinese workers are described in the following chapter.

Boat Works

The Fraser River skiffs in use during the 1880s were simply designed so that anyone with an aptitude for carpentry could build them in any shed, back yard or riverbank. One of the first boat builders in Richmond was Nathan Woodward. He was assisted by Michael Clarke, a carpenter by trade, who became the second reeve of Richmond.

Japanese immigrants, many of whom were shipwrights in their homeland, started building fishing boats for the Fraser River salmon fishery. They probably fished during the summer and built Fraser River skiffs on cannery premises during the winter when there was little opportunity for other employment. The Japanese found suitable cedar logs drifting in the river and whip-sawed these into lumber. They finished the rough lumber with a draw plane and fashioned knees and elbows from appropriately shaped driftwood. Their painted skiffs could not be distinguished from those made with lumber purchased from sawmills. These skiffs sold for $26 compared to $45-$50 for those built by Woodward. According to early pioneer Tomekichi Homma, Kyuzo Kawamura was the first Japanese to take up boat building. He was building boats on the Phoenix Cannery premises in the 1880s.

Fishing Boats

While some Native fishermen fished from their dug-out canoes, Fraser River skiffs dominated by the late 1880s. These skiffs could carry greater loads and were more stable than the dugout canoes. The skiffs had lap strake sides, flat bottoms and pointed bows and sterns. They were propelled primarily by oars, but also equipped with detachable masts and sails. Their masts were only rigged when winds were favourable for sailing. These skiffs were approximately 20 feet in length, 5 feet in width and 2.5 feet in depth. They were relatively easy to propel with oars, but difficult to sail and not very safe in rough seas. Consequently, they were adequate for fishing in the river, but unsatisfactory for the mouth of the river and beyond. Old-timers recalled that when storms whipped up at the river's mouth, many skiffs were swamped and others tossed together and smashed to match sticks.

Most of the skiffs were owned by the canning companies. After the fishing season ended, skiffs were hauled out of the water and stored on cannery premises for the winter. The boat boss repaired and painted the skiffs before the start of the following season. He covered large cracks in their cedar planks with pieces of canvas soaked in white lead and boiled linseed oil. Then he covered the canvas with tin sheets, held in place with copper tacks. He repainted the skiffs with the company's colours for easy identification on the fishing grounds. He made paint by mixing linseed oil, turpentine, white and red lead and dyes to obtain the desired colours. He used coal tar for black paint.

Fishing Nets

The original gillnets were woven of flax, which was stronger and longer lasting than cotton. Linen gillnets were first used around 1870 by Alexander Ewen's cannery near New Westminster. These nets were especially effective at night and when the Fraser River water became murky in June, July and August. Short lengths of gillnet were fished originally from Native canoes and later from flat-bottomed river skiffs.

The gillnets were made by Native women in the spring before the start of the fishing season. After the Native families arrived at the cannery, the net boss gave each woman a small quantity of linen twine, imported from Ireland, to knot. The woman held a wooden gauge in her left hand and a wooden net needle loaded

A fisherman delivering fish to the Garry Point Cannery from a Fraser River skiff. (ca. 1890) (HS)

with twine in her right hand. She made meshes by looping the needle around the gauge, picking up the mesh from the previous row and tying a double knot on the mesh. The webbing was either 45 or 60 meshes, depending upon the required depth.

After her supply of twine was exhausted, the woman returned the webbing to the net boss. He inspected the webbing to ensure the meshes were the correct size, and measured its length with a fathom stick. He paid the woman by the length of webbing she had completed, and gave her another supply of twine to make more webbing. Some women from the Musqueam band stayed in their villages near the cannery throughout the year making gillnet webbing.

Gillnets were about 150 fathoms long (900 feet) and between two and three fathoms deep. When they were used for fishing, they hung vertical in the water, supported by a "cork line" of floating elliptical cedar corks along the top and a "lead line" of small, flat, lead weights along the bottom. A net cost about one dollar per fathom for materials and labour, so each net cost about $150 to make.

When enough webbing for a net had been made, the net boss knotted half meshes with heavy cotton twine along the entire length of both edges of the webbing to make strong selvages. He then hung the webbing onto the cork and lead lines. He first attached the cedar corks to the heavy cotton cork line by threading the line through their centre holes. Then he strung the cork line between two posts in the net house, and hung the selvage on the line, spacing the corks at regular intervals. Then he turned the net upside down, and hung the other selvage onto the lead line. Flat and later hemispheric pieces of lead were crimped onto this line at regular intervals.

The net boss was responsible for making all new nets and repairing old nets. He also maintained the cannery's nets during the fishing season. Nets were generally hung to dry on make-shift net racks on land. There were few wharves, net racks and net treatment facilities during the 1880s.

Fishermen

Most of the fishermen before 1893 were Native men (Appendix Table 2). They fished with skiffs and nets owned by the canneries. Native fishermen were paid from $2.25 to $2.50 for a 12-hour day, and boat pullers 25 cents less. Four men were needed to crew each skiff, working in two 12-hour shifts. The net boss had to see that the salaried fishermen went out each morning and evening for their daily shifts. As each crew delivered its fish to the canneries and fish scows, the fish were counted and recorded by the numbers on the crew's

Fraser River skiffs fishing off Steveston with protection booms for deflecting flotsam and ice in the right foreground. (ca. 1890) (HS)

White fishermen resting on the porch of a cannery house. Many of the fishermen, such as Walter Steves and John McElhinney were sons of early pioneers. (1890) (HS)

identification tags. These daily counts helped to estimate total catches and plan daily cannery operations.

The first Caucasian fishermen were probably settlers and their descendants eager to supplement their farming income during the short sockeye fishing season. They were soon followed by labourers from Vancouver and New Westminster and also fishermen from the Columbia River. They also fished with company skiffs and nets and were paid a salary for a 12-hour day. During the fishing season the companies generally provided either bunk houses or house boats, which were single storey bunk houses built on rafts or barges. The house boats were convenient because they could be towed by a steam tug to fishing camps at the most productive fishing grounds.

The first Japanese immigrant was Manzo Nagano, who arrived in New Westminster in 1877. He fished the Fraser River with an Italian settler. Tomekichi Homma immigrated to British Columbia about 1883, and soon after was fishing for the Phoenix Cannery. By 1885 there were about six Japanese men fishing there with company skiffs and nets, and probably with company licenses. They were paid a discounted rate per fish for use of the equipment.

Gihei Kuno entered Canada in 1887 and soon after found employment in the fledgling salmon fishery. He was amazed by the abundance of fish in this country and persuaded other fishermen from his village, Mio in Wakayama Prefecture, to follow. There were few employment opportunities in rural Japan during the 1880s, so there were many second and third sons, with no prospects of inheriting the family property, willing to emigrate overseas to make their fortunes. Most early immigrants were only interested in making enough money in Canada to ensure a comfortable future life in Japan. They generally found employment as cheap labour in the fishing, lumber and mining industries.

Maps of part of the Steveston waterfront showing canneries, and Native and Chinese living quarters in 1895 and 1897. (BL)

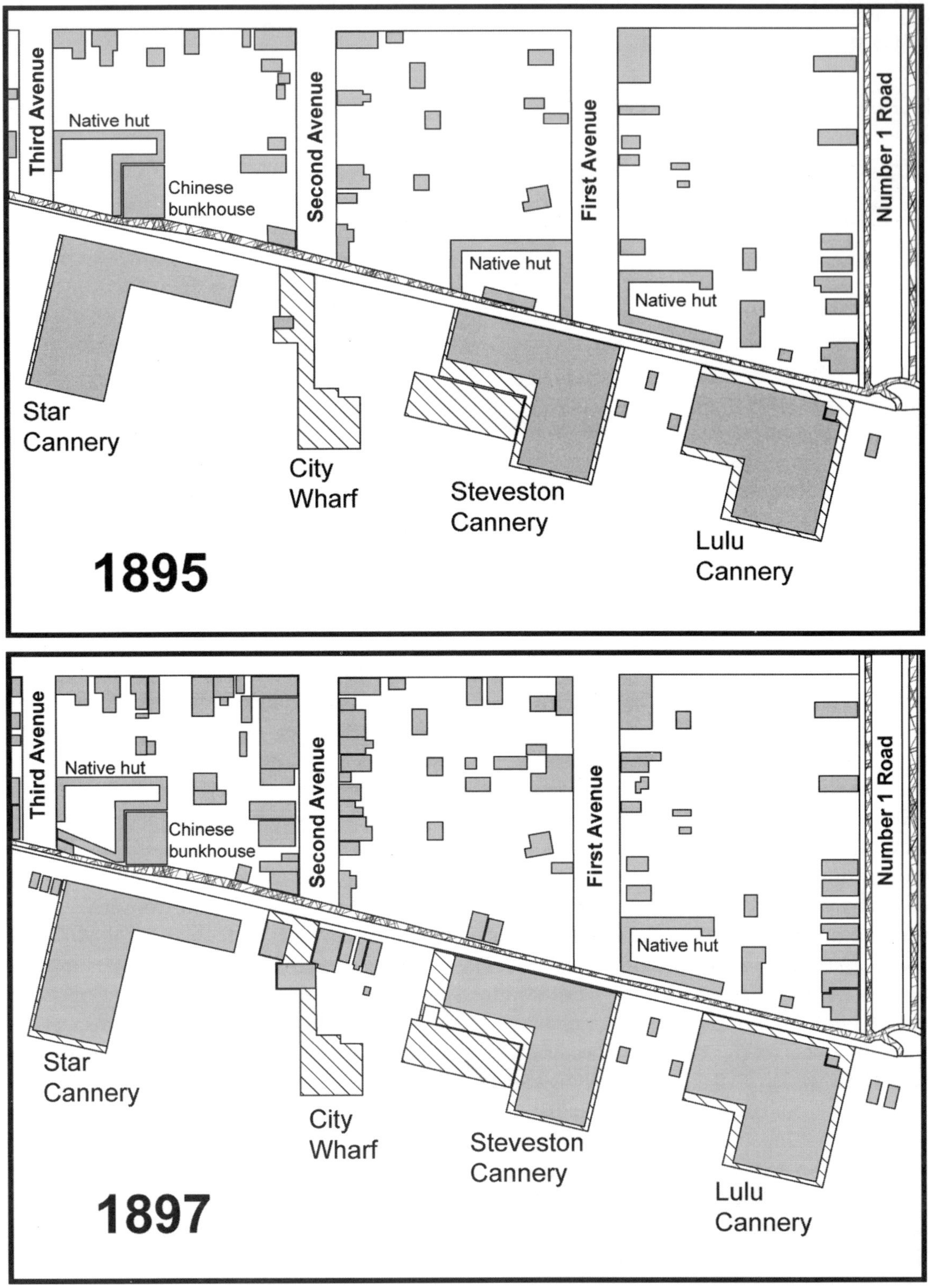

The Years of Expansion

Chapter

3

1890 - 1899

Main Channel of the Fraser River

Silt and sediment carried by the Fraser River tended to accumulate on the south side of the South Arm, enlarging Woodwards Slough and Roberts Bank and silting in Canoe Pass and Black Buoy Channel. The latter decreased in importance as the main navigation route up the river. Another larger channel developed north of Black Buoy Channel. This new channel gained prominence for navigation after the devastating flood of 1894.

Town Site and Waterfront

Many new businesses and fifteen new canneries were built along the Steveston waterfront in the 1890s. Williams' directory for 1891 lists 12 small businesses in Steveston, and Henderson's directory for 1898 lists 33. Most of these businesses were concentrated along Second Avenue, and all of them were owned by Caucasians.

The Steveston Post Office with its own post mark was founded on May 1, 1890. W.H. Steves was appointed the first Postmaster. This post office served Steveston until it became a sub-post office on May 13, 1972.

In 1891 the New Westminster and Burrard Inlet Telephone Company completed a telephone line from Steveston to Vancouver. J. C. Forlong's general store on Second Avenue received the telephone number "Steveston 1". Other enterprises in the Steveston area soon connected to this line, including the Phoenix Cannery, the Garry Point Cannery and the Steveston police station built in 1893 on Third Avenue near Chatham Street. Herbert Drummond was the first constable, and his successor Alex Mann was murdered by three Chinese men in 1900. John Dennis O'Neil became Steveston's first fire chief in 1897. Steveston had its own newspaper from 1890 to 1894, the STEVESTON ENTERPRISE, edited by M. Whitney.

Suppliers of construction materials established outlets in Steveston to take advantagc of thc building boom. After W.H. Steves sold 165 lots at a well-attended auction sale on June 18, 1891, H. A. Davis opened a

A view of Second Avenue from Bayview Street, with the Richmond Hotel in the left foreground, Forlong's general store in the right foreground and the Methodist Mission in right background. (1895) (CVA)

paint store on First Avenue, ever ready to paint the town red, the most common colour for bunkhouses. Hosea A. Bull opened a lumber yard at the southeast corner of Moncton and Number One Road, and S. J. Wescott started a brick yard with a large stock of bricks, sand and cement, barged in by scow.

Many new churches were erected. St. Anne's Anglican Church was built on Second Avenue in 1892. The Methodists held church services in the Steveston Opera House on the southwest corner of Second Avenue and Chatham Street after 1890, but Presbyterians continued to use the London's Landing Church until 1906. Alfred Green had travelled and preached to the Native people on the Nass and Skeena Rivers in northern British Columbia for thirteen years. In 1893 Green got $300 from the Missionary Society, and organized volunteers to build the Steveston Methodist Indian Mission on the northeast corner of Chatham and Second Avenue in time for the 1894 fishing season. During the summer the few Caucasian people attending the services sat on chairs on the platform behind the preacher while the Natives filled the rest of the church. About the same time Matsutaro Okamoto began holding Methodist services for the Japanese fishermen in Steveston. However, most of the fishermen and cannery workers were more interested in the saloons and gambling dens than church services.

A ditch and dike were dug by hand along the perimeter of the town site in 1891 and eventually extended to Number Two Road. The river side of the dike was fortified by a bulkhead of pilings buttressed with vertical board and batten, and a boardwalk was built on top of the dike. Plank roads were also laid on First to Sixth Avenues.

*The ferry **TRANSFER** carrying passengers, mail and freight between Steveston, Ladner and New Westminster. (ca. 1900)(HS)*

Number Two Road was graded with gravel, and Number Nine Road was paved with fir planks from Fourth Avenue to Number Three Road. Plank roads were preferred, because they were quicker to build, and mud or gravel roads became like soup after rains.

After the Marpole Bridges connected Lulu Island, Sea Island and the mainland in 1889, several stage lines were operating from Steveston to Vancouver. Among them were Freeman Steeves' Vancouver and Steveston Stage Company, Gus Wescott's Sockeye Stables and Billy Steeves' Palace Livery, Stage and Sales Stables. A round trip took an entire day to complete and cost one dollar on weekdays, two dollars on Sundays.

Settlers on the south side of Lulu Island still conducted most of their business with New Westminster rather than Vancouver. The Queensborough Bridge between the eastern end of Lulu Island and New Westminster was completed in 1892, but ferries continued to be an important mode of travel during this period. The ferry ***TELEPHONE***, and later the ferry ***EDGAR*** conducted daily runs between London's Landing, Westham Island, Ladner and New Westminster, transporting passengers, produce and merchandise. The Canadian Pacific Railway Company usurped this service in 1898 with the ***TRANSFER*** by offering lower fares for passengers and freight. Twice a week the steamer ***PRINCESS LOUISE*** travelled between New Westminster, Steveston and Victoria, and three times a week the steamer ***DUNSMUIR*** proceeded from Vancouver to Steveston to Nanaimo.

First Steveston School

Many parents complained of the one-and-one-half mile walk to English School at Number Two Road along roads that were at best planked, and at worst just ruts in the mud, or trails through brush along a slough bank. After the population of Steveston increased, school classes were held in the Opera House, in a small building once used for an ice cream parlour on Fourth Avenue, and in the Methodist Indian Mission. In 1897 Steveston's first real school, a one-room building painted yellow, was built at Second Avenue and Georgia Street where Lord Byng is today.

Merchant Sailing Ships

Steveston became an important port-of-call for merchant sailing ships during this decade. The Hudson's Bay Company clipper ship ***TITANIA*** was the first sailing ship to load cargo in Steveston for transport to Europe. In August 1889 the Bell-Irving and Patterson company contracted the ***TITANIA*** to take a shipment of canned salmon from Steveston to London. The ship docked at the Britannia wharf while the cannery was still under construction, loaded the cases of salmon, and left on September 28, 1889. It stopped briefly in Victoria and arrived in London after a 104-day trip. Before this trip all imports essential for the fishing industry, such as lead, tin plate, gillnets and machinery, were channelled through Victoria. The cases of canned salmon produced in Steveston had to be transferred by stern wheelers to Victoria before shipment to European markets. Exporting canned salmon directly from Steveston reduced costs of transportation, insurance and labour.

By 1895 the canneries in Steveston were producing approximately 200,000 cases of canned salmon. That same year, in one week, there were fourteen windjammers waiting off Steveston to load canned salmon for world markets.

Wooden-hulled sailing ships loading salmon or lumber preferred freshwater moorages to clear wood-boring teredos from their hulls, rather than Vancouver's saltwater docks. The merchant sailing ships began arriving in Steveston in late summer and continued through autumn. As these ships did not have auxiliary power, they often had to wait several days for a high tide and westerly breeze to sail from Sand Heads at the Fraser River's mouth to the Steveston waterfront. The first few days after arrival, the crew unloaded the ballast from the ship's hold. Many of the rocks used for the early dikes and road beds came from ballast taken from places around the world. The hold was then filled with cases of salmon, and the ship prepared for the return to England. The trip around Cape Horn took up to four months.

When seal hunting was in its heyday in the late 1880s and early 1890s, Steveston was one of the home ports for the sealing fleet. These schooners followed the annual migrations of the fur seal, beginning off the Oregon coast in February, then travelling along the British Columbia coast in March and April, up to the Gulf of Alaska in summer, and on the Bering Sea from August to October. Some of these schooners returned to Victoria with

Sailing ships loading canned salmon, and the ferry ***TRANSFER*** *steaming up cannery row. From the right, the Brunswick, London, Lighthouse and Star Canneries. (ca. 1900) (VMM)*

Cannery row: from the right, the Britannia, Phoenix and Dumfries, London and Garry Point Canneries, and the prominant spruce tree at Garry Point. (ca. 1890) (CVA)

loads of 1,000 to 1,500 seal skins worth about $7 each. A few of the larger schooners continued their hunt to the Russian and Japanese coasts, then sailed across the North Pacific Ocean to Oregon.

Local shipwrights repaired some of the schooners, and built their 18-foot double-ended hunting dories. Captain Atkinson, a Steveston resident whose right hand had been replaced with a hook after an accident at sea, skippered one of the sealing schooners.

Development of the Commercial Fishery

The Fraser River commercial gillnet fishery was developing rapidly. In 1892 both the cannery owners and the fishermen persuaded the federal government to rescind its regulation limiting the number of fishing licenses. The number of licensed fishing boats exploded from 500 to 2,722 in 1899. This increase ultimately resulted in the transfer of licenses to independent fishermen. Fishing started when the Sunday night gun was fired at 6:00 pm, and continued for five and a half days to 6:00 am Saturday. Many fishermen would catch the limit of 400 sockeye within the first hour. Tourists would go out to Steveston to see the great floating city of sailing skiffs or "mosquito fleet".

Meanwhile, the Americans fishing in Puget Sound were perfecting fish traps, which were banned in Canada. Landings of Fraser River sockeye by United States fisheries increased from 5 percent to 56 percent of the total during this decade (Appendix Table 1). The total Fraser River catch increased from 8.3 million in 1893 to 16.9 million in 1897, both dominant cycle years. The catches of sockeye for the off -years averaged 4.8 million fish per year.

Canneries and Other Waterfront Enterprises

Sockeye salmon were plentiful in dominant years. Even with catch limits imposed on the fishing boats, canneries often were not able to process all the salmon. Rumours of big profits and belief in an unlimited salmon resource started a stampede of investors eager to stake their dreams on the salmon industry. A major proportion of these businessmen were Scotsmen with lesser numbers of Americans, Englishmen, Swedes, Finns, Jews, Irishmen and Chinese.

In 1891 the Anglo British Columbia Packing Company Limited (ABC Company), organized by Henry Ogle Bell-Irving, paid $300,000 for nine of the twenty-six canneries in British Columbia. The company hired Marshall English to supervise the Garry Point Cannery, the Phoenix Cannery, and the Britannia Cannery in Steveston. This purchase made the ABC Company the largest in British Columbia, producing about one-quarter of all the province's canned salmon.

Fifteen canneries were built along the Steveston waterfront during this decade. Most of these canneries were L-shaped structures. Fish cutting was typically done in the short wings, and can filling in the long wings of the canneries. These canneries ranged in size from 16,000 to 70,000 square feet of floor space, including lofts and wharves, and averaged 25,000 square feet. The cannery buildings were large, plain, wooden structures with many skylights and windows. They generally had lofts for storing empty cans and nets, and making cans. At the Britannia and Phoenix Canneries a separate building parallel to the cannery was used for can-making and storage. The walls were usually made of rough board and batten, though some were of drop siding. The roofs were made of cedar shingles.

Each cannery wharf had a protection boom along its upstream side to deflect ice and debris. These booms were logs chained end to end with one end secured on land. The booms were strung between pairs of pilings, spaced at regular intervals along the length of the boom.

The capital required to start a cannery was approximately $40,000. Of this total, $25,000 was for land, buildings, and machinery, $2,000 for boats (50 X $40), $9,000 for gillnets (60 X $150) and $4,000 for steam tugs and scows. An additional $48,000 was required as working capital to put up the season's pack of canned salmon.

The chart tells the number of licenses, cannery workers, and 48-pound cases packed by the four canneries that operated on the Steveston waterfront in 1890.

Cannery	Number of boat licenses	Number of workers	Cases packed
English	22	290	20,917
Garry Point	18	240	15,106
Beaver	18	205	14,253
Britannia	17	192	12,753
Total	75	927	63,029

The number of operating canneries on the Steveston waterfront increased to eleven in 1895, and fifteen in 1899. The cannery owners formed the B.C. Salmon Packers Association in 1898 to control labour and fish costs. Many of the canneries were operated for only a few years. They are listed below in chronological order:

Britannia Cannery (1890)

Construction of this cannery was started in 1889 and completed the following year by William Archibald Duncan, J. Bachelor and Eli Harrison. It was purchased by Henry Ogle Bell-Irving in 1890 and became part of the ABC Company purchase in 1891. William R. Lord became manager. This plant with one canning line was operated by the ABC company until 1918, when it was converted into a shipyard which repaired the boats of the ABC Company fleet, mainly their larger seiners and fish packers. In 1969 the ABC Company sold the Britannia Shipyard to the

Cannery row: from the left, the Garry Point Cannery, the public wharf with shed, the London, Phoenix, Britannia and Beaver Canneries with a Fraser River skiff in the foreground. (ca. 1890) (NWPL)

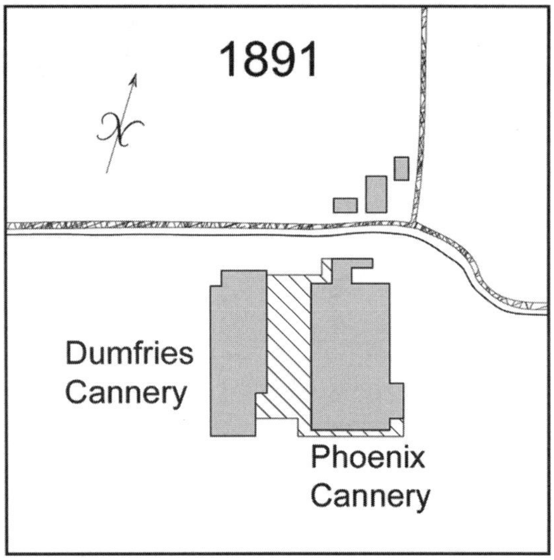

General plan of the Phoenix and Dumfries Canneries. (BL)

Canadian Fishing Company, which operated it until 1979, and then sold it to the British Columbia Packers Association (BC Packers). The City of Richmond was given 8.4 acres including the Britannia buildings in exchange for higher density on the remaining two acres of the site in 1990. The Britannia Heritage Shipyard Society was registered in 1991 to preserve the site. This shipyard was declared a national historic site by the National Historic Sites and Monuments Board in 1992.

(Lulu Island) London Cannery (1891)

This cannery was built by the Lulu Island Canning Company, owned by J.J. Crane, Benjamin J. Short, George S. Dutcher and William McPherson. It operated from 1891 to 1895, when it was purchased by the London Canning Company of John H. Turner, Robert Arthur, Lawrence Kirk and G.A. Kirk, and renamed the London. It was operated from 1897 to 1901, when it was purchased and converted to a warehouse by BC Packers. The building was demolished before 1911, as the fire insurance map for that year showed a public wharf at this site. This wharf was used by merchant ships to load lumber destined for overseas markets. The Columbia Cold Storage was built on this site in 1915.

Dumfries Cannery (1891)

This was a "dummy" cannery built in 1891 by the ABC Company to qualify for 20 fishing licenses assigned to each cannery. A photograph taken about 1885 showed only the Phoenix Cannery with its lower foreshore end. A later photograph taken about 1891 showed another higher building immediately downstream of the Phoenix Cannery. On the

Maps of the Steveston waterfront showing locations of the canneries in 1895 and additional canneries in 1897. (solid buildings - operating: clear building - not operating) (BL)

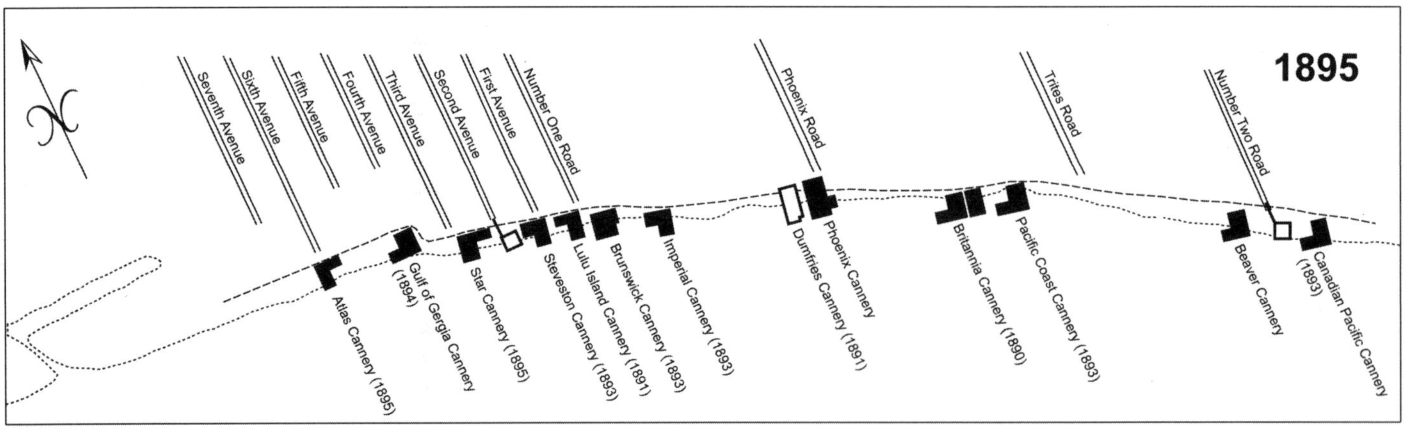

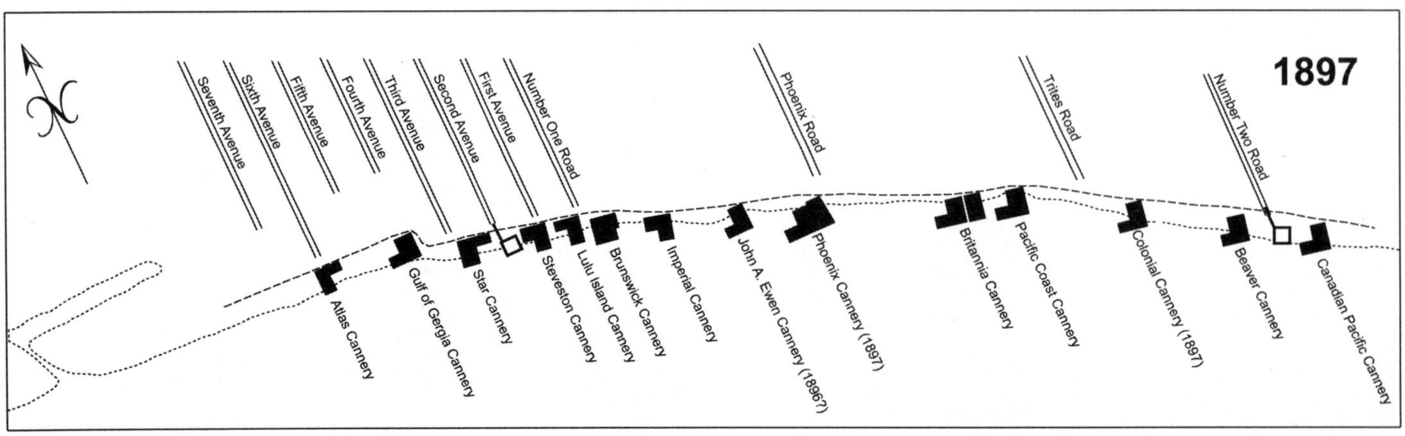

1895 fire insurance map there were two parallel buildings on the site. The downstream building was the Dumfries Cannery and the upstream one was the Phoenix. Both the Dumfries Cannery and the Phoenix Cannery were destroyed by fire on July 3, 1895.

(Ewen) Hume Cannery (1891)

Alexander Ewen and Company erected this "dummy", most probably to qualify for fishing licenses. The fire insurance map for 1897 showed the Ewen cannery at a site midway between the Phoenix Cannery and the Imperial Cannery, whereas the map for 1911 showed the John A. Hume Cannery at the same location. Hume evidently purchased this cannery from Ewen and put it in operation from 1896 through 1902. This cannery was purchased by BC Packers, and used for net storage until it was demolished some time after 1936.

Pacific Coast Cannery (1893)

This cannery was built east of the Britannia Cannery by the Pacific Coast Packing Company of George Wilson, George Cassady and Ninian Bain. It was commonly referred to as the "Ben" Cannery by the Japanese. It was operated through 1905, and after this date only every fourth year during the dominant sockeye salmon runs. Also purchased by BC Packers in 1902, this cannery was used as a herring saltery from 1918 to 1930. The last of the old L-shaped canneries, it was later used as a seine net and gillnet storage shed for BC Packers fishermen. It was demolished by the federal government in 1997.

Imperial Cannery (1893)

This cannery was built by Benjamin J. Short and W.H. Squair on a site east of Number One Road and the "Little Slough". It was operated from 1893 to 1896. The cannery was not operated in 1897, and was sold the following year to Robert Ward and Company, and in 1902 to BC Packers. The original cannery was replaced with a larger building at the same site combined with the Brunswick Cannery. The canning machinery from the Brunswick, Hume and Imperial Canneries was combined to create a new Imperial plant with four canning lines, the largest cannery in the British Empire. The new Imperial Cannery was operated every year from 1903 through 1992, and was the last cannery to can salmon on the Steveston waterfront.

The Britannia Cannery with gillnets drying on net racks on the partially planked wharf. (ca. 1900)(CRA)

The Pacific Coast Cannery with Columbia River type boats, a fish scow and fishermen loading a bluestone tank in the foreground. (1908) (CVA)

(Steveston) Lighthouse Cannery (1893)

This cannery was built at the foot of First Avenue by the Steveston Canning Company of Michael Costello, R.A. McMorran and Ed Hunt. It was operated by this company from 1893 to 1895. The cannery was purchased and renamed the Lighthouse Cannery by the Federation Salmon Canning and Packing Company of Walter Morris, Samuel Okell and Alexander J. McLellan in 1896. The Lighthouse Cannery was not operated after 1905. It was destroyed in the great Steveston fire of 1918.

Canadian Pacific Cannery (1893)

This cannery was founded by George Alexander, R.V. Winch and Dave S. Hennessey on a site east of Number Two Road. Caucasians referred to it as the "Red Cannery" because of its colour, and Japanese called it the "Winch Cannery". Over twenty years earlier in 1870 Dave Hennessey and Alexander Ewen had started the first salmon cannery in British Columbia at Annieville near New Westminster. Hennessey and Winch sold their shares in the Canadian Pacific Cannery to Alexander Ewen in 1896, and BC Packers purchased the cannery in 1902. The cannery was operated from 1893 through 1905. After this date it was operated only during the dominant sockeye salmon runs of 1909, 1913, and 1917. The cannery was destroyed by fire in 1924.

Brunswick Cannery (1893)

Benjamin J. Short and W.H. Squair hired Dave Mackie to construct this cannery at the foot of Number One Road west of the "Little Slough". However, they soon sold the cannery to the Brunswick Canning Company of George Dawson, Alfred J. Buttimer and George I. Wilson. The cannery was operated from 1893 through 1902, when it was one of 35 canneries consolidated by BC Packers. After 1902 it was used as a warehouse for the Imperial Cannery.

Gulf of Georgia Cannery (1894)

After the Garry Point Cannery was damaged by erosion, Charles Windsor bought it back from the ABC Company for $5,000 in 1893, and rebuilt the cannery in 1894. The following year the cannery ownership was transferred to the Malcolm and Windsor Company of Oswald M. Malcolm, Charles S. Windsor and George I. Wilson. It was called the Malcolm and Windsor Cannery, or the Gulf of Georgia Cannery. The owners added a second canning line, making it the largest cannery on the coast, a distinction retained until the Imperial was rebuilt in 1902. The Canadian Fishing Company (CanFisCo) bought the cannery in 1926 and operated it until 1930. The cannery was shut down during the 1930s, but was operated from 1940 to 1946 to can herring. From 1940 to 1966 a reduction plant there processed herring into oil and fish meal. Overfishing forced the herring fishery to close between 1967 and 1971. From 1972 to 1979 the reduction plant processed by-products from the herring roe fishery. Later the plant was used for net and gear storage.

In 1976 the Historic Sites and Monuments Board designated the Gulf of Georgia Cannery a national historic site. The cannery was purchased by the Department of Fisheries and Oceans and leased back to CanFisCo in 1977. It was then transferred to the Canadian Parks Service in 1984, and operated jointly by the Gulf of Georgia Cannery Society and Parks Canada as a National Historic Site. Canfisco continued to operate the adjacent seine net loft.

Atlas Cannery (1895)

This cannery was built by Andrew Houston and Partners at the foot of Sixth Avenue. It was purchased by BC Packers in the amalgamation of 1902. It was operated during eight of the eleven years to 1905. The cannery was destroyed and replaced by a storage shed some time after 1911. BC Packers sold this site in 1931 and purchased it again in 1935. The site was used as a fish camp for part of the BC Packers' gillnet fleet until the 1980s. The Steveston Harbour Authority developed a wharf for offshore trawlers at this location.

Star Cannery (1895)

The Star Packing Company of Michael Costello and R.A. McMorran completed this cannery at the foot of Third Avenue early in 1895. It was demolished by fire in May, but was rebuilt in time for the 1895 season. The cannery was purchased by the Canadian Canning Company of R.E. Gosse in 1899, and operated through 1909. The disastrous fire that consumed three blocks of Steveston from Number One Road to Third Avenue in May 1918 also destroyed the Star Cannery. This site was purchased by the Gosse-Millerd Company in 1921 and subsequently by several other companies. BC Packers purchased the property in 1935, and sold the portion inside the dyke. The portion outside was retained and was later used as a fish camp for part of the BC Packers gillnet fleet.

Hong Wo General Store (1895)

This store was a prominent feature of the Steveston waterfront for almost a century. "Hong Wo" means "living in harmony". Ling Chung Lam built the store along the waterfront between Trites Road and the Phoenix Cannery

The Canadian Pacific Cannery with net racks and Columbia River type boats in the foreground. (ca. 1910) (CRA)

The Scottish Canadian Cannery complex with the cannery houses and bunkhouses on the right. (1908)(VPL)

The Gulf of Georgia Cannery with a gasoline engine powered boat on the left for towing gillnetters to and from the fishing grounds, a larger steam engine-powered boat for collecting fish with fish scows, and a fish scow at moorage on the right. (ca. 1900)(CVA)

in 1895 to serve the fishing and farming communities of the area. The store was so well stocked with hardware, clothing, dry goods, vegetables, fruits and meats that it was called Richmond's first supermarket. At the height of its popularity before World War II, there were as many as eight clerks catering to customers. The store was especially convenient for fishermen as it was built over the river on pilings, and they could tie directly to its wharf. Also, Lam devised an order list specifically for fishermen to check off the hardware and provisions they needed each week. Lam owned one hundred acres of nearby farm land on which Chinese labourers grew vegetables. He also operated several greenhouses and a pickling plant on his farm. He retailed some of the produce from his farm and greenhouses through the Great West Vegetable Market on Granville Street. After 1914 Lam acted as a contractor and provided Chinese workers to the Phoenix and Britannia Canneries. These workers were boarded in the three bunkhouses built around the general store. On the ground floor of one of the bunkhouses was the cookhouse containing a massive brick fireplace with openings for four woks or cauldrons. Chinese workers continued to live in the bunkhouse in front of the store till the 1950s. The general store was closed in 1971 and the store and bunkhouses were demolished by the Richmond Municipality in 1977.

Phoenix Cannery (1897)

After fire destroyed the Phoenix Cannery and Dumfries Cannery in 1895, the ABC Company built the new Phoenix Cannery immediately west of the site of the original Phoenix Cannery in time for the 1897 fishing season. This new cannery was a L-shaped building with another building beside it for can storage. The Phoenix was the second longest operating cannery on the Steveston waterfront, canning salmon for 72 years. It closed in the spring of 1969 after the ABC Company sold the cannery to CanFisCo. In 1979 BC Packers acquired the property. The empty Phoenix

The boardwalk along the wooden dyke leading to the Hong Wo general store complex, Natives in a dugout canoe, and Columbia River type boats at moorage. (1905)(VPL)

Cannery was partially burned in August 1997, after being inoperative for several years.

Colonial Cannery (1897)

This cannery with one canning line was constructed by the Colonial Canning Company, owned by Isaac Church, Robert Hampton, Thomas Hood, Hezekiah Stead and William J. Sproeklin, at a site downstream of the Beaver Cannery. It was sold in 1898 to the William Farrell's Columbia Packing Company, in 1901 to the Kwong Man Tai Company owned by Lee Yine and Lee Poon Kai, and in 1902 to BC Packers. It was operated from 1897 through 1903 and in 1905. In 2005 it was one of three original 1890s canneries still remaining on the waterfront, and was used as a gillnet storage shed.

Scottish Canadian Cannery (1899)

This cannery was built by the Malcolm and Windsor United Canning Company over the tidal flats northwest of Garry Point. It was transferred to the Scottish Canadian Canning Company Limited owned by J. W. Windsor, O. G. Malcolm, Frank Burnett, J. J. Crane and J. E. McRae. It was unique because it remained one-quarter of a mile outside the new dyke built in 1906. The entire cannery complex was built on pilings, including cannery houses, bunkhouses, wharves and net racks. This plant with two canning lines was operated until about 1912. Gillnet fishermen and their families continued to live in the cannery houses until the Japanese evacuation in 1942. The cannery buildings and houses disappeared some time in the 1940s, and the boardwalk and wharf in the early 1950s.

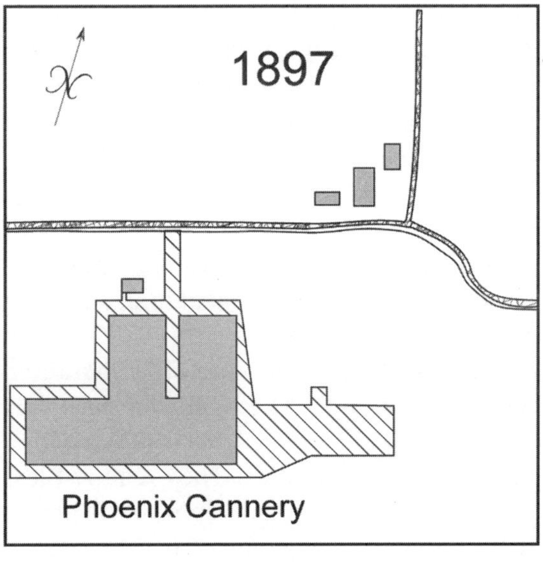

General plan of the Phoenix Cannery in 1897. (BL)

The interior of a cannery showing systems of shafts, pulleys and belts used to power machinery and to move materials between stations. (ca. 1900)(HS)

Canning Operations

Salmon canning continued to be highly labour intensive during this period, with minor improvements, but no major breakthroughs in labour-saving devices. A few machines were harnessed to steam power with a system of shafts, pulleys and belts. Materials moved more easily between stations on conveyor belts. The steam box further reduced cooking time. Cans were treated in the steam box for only a few minutes to vent air in the cans, and then sealed prior to their final cooking in the retorts. These technological changes increased the production of a 120- to 150-man crew from 1,000 cases in 1883 to 1,200 cases in 1893.

Of the fifteen new canneries, twelve were one-line canneries. Only the Phoenix, Gulf of Georgia and Scottish Canadian had two canning lines. Multiple-line canneries were probably more difficult to manage because of their larger multi-racial work force. The one-line cannery was more efficient in an industrial era based on manpower.

Half-pound cans were first marketed during this decade. These smaller cans cost more in labour to produce, but sold at a higher price per unit of product. They required less time in the steam box and retort, so that more fish could be processed in a day.

A case of 48 one-pound cans of salmon cost between $3.50 and $4.00 to produce in the early 1890s. This included $1.00 for fish (10 fish at $0.10 each), $0.50 to $0.75 for Chinese labour, $0.67 for cans, $0.33 for solder, $0.16 for wood boxes, $0.24 for labels and $0.60 to $0.85 miscellaneous.

Cannery Workers

The labour force continued to be dominated by Native women on the washing and can-filling stations and Chinese men in all other aspects of cannery work except the managerial, technical and supervisory tasks.

Henry Doyle, the founder and first general manager of BC Packers, left a detailed list of the workers required to crew a canning line capable of packing 1,000 cases of flats or 600 cases of half-flats in a day's operation. This list was made in 1904, before the introduction of significant labour saving technologies, and it demonstrated the numbers and kinds of workers needed to operate a salmon cannery at the turn of the century (See Chart).

Between 120 and 150 workers were required to crew a canning line. Therefore the eighteen canning lines operated by the fifteen canneries on the Steveston waterfront in 1899 would have required between 2,200 and 2,700 workers. An additional 5,400 men were needed to crew the licensed fishing boats. These estimates do not include people engaged in the service industry that catered to fishermen and cannery workers during the salmon fishing season.

The fire insurance map of the Steveston waterfront for 1897 gave population estimates of 6,000 in summer and 400 in winter. Doyle estimated 6,000 to 8,000 fishing industry workers in Steveston during the summer. Thus the summer population of transient workers in Steveston was up to twenty times as big as the resident winter population.

To house these large multi-racial groups of workers, companies built segregated housing near the canneries. Native workers lived in long, single-story, multiple-family units. The fire insurance map of the Steveston waterfront for 1895 showed three of these housing units along the waterfront between Number One Road and Third Avenue. Only two remained by 1897, and both were gone by 1911. This reflected the decreasing number of Native workers in the Fraser River salmon canning industry during the late 1890s, as Natives sought employment in the new salmon

Nationality	Numbers	Duties
Caucasian	6	(foreman, fish tallyman, machine lineman, bathroom man, engineer/ fireman, bookkeepr/storekeeper)
Chinese	50-62	(fish cutters, fish picklers, trucking fish, fish slitting machine, carrying fish to fillers, ticket punchers, filling light cans, carrying fish to wiper, feeding wiper, carrying cans to salting machine, feeding tops, crimper, solder machine, cooler fillers, stopping off, cold test, mending leaks, bathroom, lye kettle)
Native women	55-85	(filling, in gut shed)

canneries constructed along the central and north coasts. Also, an influx of Japanese men in the 1890s and Japanese women in the early 1900s greatly increased the numbers of fishermen and cannery workers available to the Fraser River canneries.

Cannery Houses

Bunkhouses for cannery workers and fishermen were often "knockdowns" that were built at the New Westminster sawmills, then disassembled or "knocked down". The walls and floors were loaded flat on scows for delivery. After they arrived at Steveston, the buildings were quickly reconstructed by

Chinese workers testing cans for faulty seals between the initial cooking and the final cooking. (1908) (VPL)

resident carpenters, giving the appearance of small villages rising at each cannery almost overnight. The one-storey and one-and-one-half storey bunkhouses were built with balloon-type construction. The outside wall studs of the latter were 14 feet long, reaching a height of one-and-one-half storeys. As the walls were raised up, the floor joists for the upper floor were nailed directly to the wall studs 10 feet up. Two of these bunkhouses were restored at the Britannia Shipyard.

Canneries generally had "China houses" on their premises to house the Chinese workers. The Chinese crews ranged from 70 for a small cannery to between 150 and 200. These bunkhouses were barn-like buildings with two storeys. Smaller bunkhouses were about 24 feet by 40 feet, but some were as large as 50 feet by 50 feet, housing up to 100 Chinese workers.

On the ground floor a row of rooms along one side was filled with three-tiered bunks. The bottoms of the bunks were one-by-twelve boards. The remaining space served as the eating area and common room. A wood stove in this open room was the only source of heat. The upper floor was filled with bunks and occasionally partitioned into small rooms. These bunkhouses were designed to accommodate the greatest number of persons without any regard for comfort or privacy. Occupants often built their own cubicles around their bunks, with whatever materials they were able to scrounge.

The kitchen was often a lean-to on the back of the bunkhouse, although it was sometimes located on the main floor. The brickwork stove extended along the length of the room and had up to five round fireplace openings on top. Cordwood, cut in four-foot lengths and split in half, was used as fuel for this stove. Large, iron woks or cauldrons, which fit into the fireplace openings, were used for cooking and boiling water. The workers were fed three meals on working days and only two meals on other days. The staple diet was rice, fish and cabbage. Pork or chicken was included in the diet once a week at most.

The bunkhouses generally had outdoor fireplaces with improvised water tanks. These were heated most of the time to provide hot water for washing. The sides of coal oil cans were cut out to make small tubs for taking towel baths.

Chinese workers often had ample free time on their hands during periods of poor

Native huts behind the Star Cannery with a Chinese bunkhouse on the left. (ca. 1895)(HS)

Native fishermen and cannery workers in front of cannery houses. (ca. 1905)(NWPL)

fishing, on weekends, and after work. They spent this free time in the bunkhouse because there were few places for them to go, and they generally had no money for entertainment. Low stake gambling games of mah-jong, pai-gow or fifteen-wu were played every night. Drinking was another popular pastime, even though early contracts stipulated that the contractor would be fined if alcohol was sold on the premises. The workers concocted potent home-brews for their own consumption and for sale to Natives. Opium, which was legal up to 1908, was supplied by the contractor. Opium addicts would crawl into their cloistered cubicles to light their pipes and escape the cares of the day. Cannery managers lived under constant threat of fires from addicts oblivious of their surroundings.

Boat Works

The first documented boat works in Steveston was operated by I. Yamamota. In 1892 he advertised in the February 3rd issue of the STEVESTON ENTERPRISE as a *"Japanese boat builder: of skiffs, sloops, fishing boats, keel boats and sealing boats. Fishing boats from $28 to $35."* The skiffs would have been the common Fraser River flat-bottomed type. The sloops, fishing boats and keel boats would probably be designed like the later Collingwood and Columbia River type boats. Chiyo Kuno (probably Gihei Kuno) was mentioned in H. O. Bell-Irving's diary as a boatbuilder working for William Lord at the Britannia Cannery in February 1895. Another early boat builder cum blacksmith in Steveston was Robert P. Carter whose enterprise was listed in Henderson's British Columbia Gazetteer and Directory for 1898 and 1899.

Fishing Boats

The round-bottomed Columbia River gillnetter was introduced in the late 1880s, and soon replaced the flat-bottomed Fraser River skiff. This boat was caravel-built, and measured about 25 feet in length, 6 feet 6 inches in breadth and 3 feet in depth. It had a sprit sail on a fixed mast in front of the centre board. It also had two sets of oarlocks, and fish holds on each side of the centre board. The longer stern section of the boat was used for net storage and handling, and the shorter

Steam tugs with fish scows for collecting fish from Fraser River skiffs. (ca. 1895)(CRA)

bow section was the living quarters. A canvas pup tent provided shelter for sleeping and some protection from rain. This boat was superior to the Fraser River skiff because it could sail better, carry a heavier load, and negotiate rougher seas. However, it was harder to propel by rowing. Each boat was crewed by two men, a fisherman and a boat puller. Canneries used steam-powered boats to tow the fishing boats to the most productive fishing grounds, and to tow scows out to collect fish from their fishing boats. The boats were manned through sun and storm from Sunday night to Saturday morning each week.

P.J. Barry attributed the introduction of the round-bottomed fishing boat to Captain William Watts. The Captain's father, William Watts Senior, was an immigrant from Ireland who started building small boats on Toronto Island in Lake Ontario. These boats were 20 feet long, clinker-built, double-ended and equipped with one or two sprit sails. Watts probably patterned this boat after vessels in his homeland. When he moved to Collingwood on Georgian Bay in Ontario a few years later, his boats gained wide popularity among fishermen. Captain William Watts and his partner Trotts moved from Collingwood to the Pacific Coast in 1888, and started a boat yard that eventually became the Vancouver Shipyard. They received an order for 100 Collingwood boats from a cannery. These boats were built bottom up over a solid mould at a rate of one per day, and soon became very popular in the fishery.

However, the Columbia River Maritime Museum asserted the round-bottomed boats were first built in San Francisco for the Sacramento River fishery in the late 1860s, and subsequently introduced into the Columbia River fishery and the Fraser River fishery in the late 1880s.

A larger version of the Columbia River boat was also built in Steveston, as fishermen

Columbia River type boats fishing off Steveston. (ca.1900) (HS)

A gasoline engine-powered boat towing Columbia River type boats to the fishing grounds. (1913)(VPL)

began to fish further out at sea. As these boats were used at Bristol Bay, Alaska, they became known as Bristol Bay boats in Seattle and Steveston. The last five boats built for use at Bristol Bay were built by Allan Steves in the early 1950s at Mike David's (Atagi) Boat Works at the Scottish Canadian Cannery site.

Wharves

As the number of boats increased, the protection booms on the upstream and offshore sides of the wharves proved useful. With a mooring line on a boom piling and another line to the wharf, a boat could be secured perpendicular rather than parallel to the wharf.

Companies built net racks and bluestone tanks for their fishermen. Linen nets required frequent repair and treatment. Most early net racks were partially decked wharves on pilings over open water. Narrow boardwalks with raised racks of wooden poles were built at regular intervals across these wharves. Fishermen hung their gillnets across the racks to dry and mend. They soaked the gillnets in copper sulphate solutions in bluestone tanks made of cedar staves.

Fishermen

Many Native fishermen left the Fraser River fishery, and the number of Caucasian and Japanese fishermen increased. After 1892 only British subjects were eligible for fishing licenses. However, American fishermen from the Columbia and Sacramento Rivers continued to fish in the Fraser River after this date, often with the assistance of the canneries. At first, few of the Japanese fishermen fulfilled the four-year residency requirement to qualify as a British subject. In 1890 fishing licenses were held by 167 "Whites" and 25 Japanese. By 1899 this had increased to 710 "Whites" and 1,361 Japanese (Appendix Table 2).

The payment schedule to fishermen was changed in 1893 from a salary for a twelve-hour day to a price per fish. Fishermen were paid six cents per sockeye in 1893 and eight cents per sockeye in 1897. Speaking to the Steveston Fishermen's Association, Tadaichi Nagao said he would have to catch 3,500 fish at eight cents each to cover his expenses for the 100 day fishing season, including $66 for the puller's wages, $100 for the net, $35 for the boat, $10 for the license, $23 for food, $7 for boots and $25 for personal expenses.

The rental fee for cannery boats and equipment was approximately one third of a fisherman's catch. This encouraged Caucasian fishermen, with greater financial resources than the Natives and Japanese, to purchase their own fishing skiffs and nets. The first independent fishermen lived in the surrounding area, and stored and maintained their own equipment.

Settlers in Richmond and Delta continued to participate in the summer salmon fishing season. The prospects of high returns also attracted Caucasians from Vancouver and New Westminster. During the fishing season single Caucasian fishermen were frequently housed

A riverside scene with Fraser River skiffs, Columbia River type boats, Native dugout canoes and a houseboat for accommodating Caucasian fishermen. (ca. 1900)(HS)

in small cabins on barges stationed near the most productive fishing grounds.

By 1898 there were about 1,300 Japanese fishermen. Although most regarded their stay as temporary, a few saw Canada as their new home, and proceeded to bring their wives, raise families and purchase property. There were only thirteen Japanese women in Steveston in 1897.

The boom in new cannery construction greatly increased the demand for fishermen. Crews for fifty to sixty boats were required to supply a cannery with enough fish. Japanese fishermen were hard working, consistently catching more fish than Caucasian and Native fishermen, and canneries actively sought their services. The industry brought in Japanese to replace Caucasian fishermen who were leaving for the gold fields of Slocan and the Yukon in the 1890s.

Accommodations for single Japanese fishermen were designed to board the maximum number of men with minimum concerns for their comfort. Thirty to sixty fishermen lived in each bunk house under the supervision of a Japanese boss. The boss negotiated with the company on their behalf, and got a commission on their catches. Each tenant was provided with a bunk in a crowded room and meals in a common mess-hall. The meals were prepared by Japanese cooks.

The fishermen had little time for recreation, and few diversions other than drinking, gambling or visiting bawdy-houses. Dozens of saloons, gambling dens and brothels prospered during the short fishing season.

Before 1897 no licenses were issued in Steveston to sell liquor. Instead, "Clubs" were established for members only to gather for camaraderie, recreation and social drinking. These clubs disappeared when three-fifths of the residents of Steveston signed a petition in favour of licensing hotels to sell liquor.

Japanese Fishermen's Benevolent Society (Gyosha Dantai)

The Japanese fishermen in Steveston organized a Fishermen's Association in 1897 with Tomekichi Homma as the first president. This association was registered as the Japanese Fishermen's Benevolent Society under the British Columbia Benevolent Society Act in 1900.

Epidemics of contagious diseases, primarily typhoid fever, swept through Steveston almost every summer until the early 1900s, because of unsanitary practices along the waterfront. River water was frequently used for washing, cooking and drinking. Canneries discarded heads, tails and guts, and even entire salmon in times of glut, into the river. Outhouses for canneries and bunkhouses

Columbia River type boats and living quarters for Japanese fishermen. (ca. 1905) (UBC-SC)

Hospital built by the Japanese Fishermen's Benevolent Society on Number One Road. (ca. 1908)(HS)

were generally built over the river. These practices made outbreaks of epidemic diseases inevitable.

Both the Chinese cannery workers and the Japanese fishermen lived in crowded, communal bunkhouses. However, the Chinese were affected less severely by typhoid fever than the Japanese, probably because the Chinese drank boiled tea and rarely ate uncooked food. The Japanese were accustomed to drinking water and eating raw vegetables and fish. While at sea, the Japanese fishermen probably used river water for drinking and cooking, in most instances without sufficient boiling because their stoves were just tin cans containing a wood or bark fire.

Dr. Umejiro Yamamura and Dr. Seinosuke Oishi, two dentists from Oregon who visited Steveston in 1895, were appalled by the living conditions of Japanese fishermen. They advised Matsutaro Okamoto, the Japanese Methodist lay minister, and Iwakichi Shimamura, a leader of the Japanese fishermen, of the pressing need to provide hospital facilities for the Japanese fishermen. Shimamura obtained the use of some land from the Phoenix Cannery, and purchased lumber from the Royal City Sawmill in New Westminster. Some fishermen volunteered their time and labour to erect a two story building with the ground level for mission activities and the upper level for the minister's living quarters. It was used immediately upon completion in 1895 to care for patients during an outbreak of typhoid. Out of 38 typhoid cases reported in 1896 in Richmond, 26 were among Japanese, and 12 among Natives. The mission was funded by contributions from Japanese fishermen. Dr. R.W. Large, a medical doctor and Methodist minister, helped run the hospital and treat the sick in 1898 and 1899. Besides serving as a hospital, the mission operated a Japanese language school and conducted religious services.

The voluntary contributions of the fishermen did not cover the operating expenses, and the mission went into debt. The Fishermen's Association asked Tatsugoro Nosse, the Japanese Consul, for assistance. At a meeting in July 1898 Consul Nosse addressed the Japanese fishermen, extolling the benefits provided by the hospital and its importance in showing Japanese commitment to the community. He urged them to take full financial responsibility for its operations. The Association collected eighteen hundred dollars to build a larger hospital on the northeast corner of Chatham Street and Number One Road in 1900. They also built a new Japanese Methodist mission across the street on the southwest corner. The new hospital had a dispensary, a clinic, a minor operating room, a general ward for more than thirty people and two small rooms for special patients. The hospital was separated from the mission, and the Japanese Fishermen's Benevolent Society assessed Japanese families eight dollars per year to cover operating costs. This nominal fee entitled participants to full medical coverage, including consultations, medicine and hospital beds, but excluding operations which had to be paid for separately. The Society initially hired Dr. R.R. Robinson, who had a practice in Steveston at the time, and two Caucasian nurses to treat the inpatients. Doctors and nurses were recruited in Japan to staff the hospital in later years. The hospital and medical insurance plan continued until the outbreak of the Second World War.

A doctor, some nurses and patients on the porch of the Japanese fishermen's hospital. (ca. 1900)(CVA)

Discrimination against Japanese Canadians

Concerned about the growing numbers of Japanese immigrants in the labour force, the Caucasian population demanded controls on Japanese immigration and restrictions on their civil liberties. The provincial government petitioned the dominion government to extend the $50 "head tax" imposed on all Chinese immigrants to the Japanese. The dominion government did not comply because Great Britain and Japan had signed the Treaty of Commerce and Navigation of 1894 pledging equal treatment of their nationals in the other's territories. The provincial government also passed an immigration act requiring all immigrants to take a language test, which would have effectively barred entry of all Japanese and Chinese. The dominion government disallowed this act, stating that under the British North America Act such a measure was beyond the jurisdiction of the provincial government. However, in 1895 the provincial government passed the provincial elections act depriving Chinese, East Indians, Japanese and Native Peoples of the right to vote in provincial elections. This act denied the vote not only to immigrants who had become British subjects, but also to all their children who were born in Canada. These people also lost the right to vote in municipal and federal elections. Moreover, this act effectively barred them from various types of employment because only people eligible to be on the voters list were permitted to work in the civil service, and to practice law and pharmacy. The provincial elections act of 1895 profoundly influenced the lives of all persons of Japanese ancestry.

Tomekichi Homma challenged this act on October 19, 1900. He applied to Thomas Cunningham, Collector of Voters for the electoral district of Vancouver, to have his name placed on the voters list. When Cunningham refused, Homma appealed to the County Court of Vancouver. Chief Justice McColl of the Supreme Court of British Columbia ruled that the clause prohibiting naturalized Japanese from voting was beyond the powers of the provincial legislature, and ordered Homma's name be entered on the voters list. This decision was sustained by the Supreme Court of Canada. The provincial government then appealed to the Privy Council, which reversed the decision on March 9, 1901. This ruling confirmed the provincial legislature's authority to deny the right of a

British subject to vote in a provincial election and to work in certain professions because of his race. This decision of the Privy Council clearly defined how the powers of the federal and provincial governments were divided under the British America Act. The provinces had exclusive jurisdiction over civil rights.

Winter Activities

The salmon canning industry was highly seasonal, requiring large numbers of workers for a relatively short period of time. Native families, Chinese labourers and Caucasian and Japanese fishermen came to Steveston during the summer to work.

During the fishing season the Steveston waterfront was a bee-hive of activity, with fishermen out on the water five and a half days and nights of the week. The canneries often operated fifteen to eighteen hours per day. Most of the fishermen and cannery workers left Steveston in September after the fishing season. The fishing boats were hauled out of the water and loaded on two hand trucks. Chinese and Japanese workers pushed the boats into the canneries. They man-handled the boats off the trucks and stacked them on their sides in long rows.

After the fishing season the Natives returned to their villages, and the Chinese to "China towns" in Vancouver, Victoria, New Westminster and Nanaimo. The Japanese returned to "Little Tokyo" along Powell Street in Vancouver to find work in the forest and mining industries. From about November to February the Steveston waterfront came to a virtual standstill with only a few cannery workers retained to repair buildings, machinery and equipment for the next fishing season. A few Japanese carpenters also remained to build boats on cannery premises.

Some of the Japanese fishermen went to Mayne Island after the sockeye salmon season to cut cordwood to fuel the boilers and make charcoal for the soldering pots. Charcoal was made by firing wood stacked in large, sealed, rock-lined pits. The wood and charcoal were shipped in schooners to the canneries. By the turn of the century, Japanese people were working on most of the Gulf Islands. An immigration officer in 1901 estimated there were several hundred Japanese cutting wood on Mayne, Pender, Prevost and Galiano Islands. When the solderless can-making machines were introduced into the salmon canning industry in the early 1900s, these charcoal operations were discontinued.

Tomekichi Homma, the first president of the Japanese Fishermen's Benevolent Association, and the first Japanese to contest the law depriving Japanese of the right to vote. (ca.1900)(C. Yasui collection)

Moncton Street, looking east from Third Avenue. This area was the main commercial centre of Steveston after the turn of the century. (1908)(VPL)

BEAVER No. 2, the dredge used to dig a 33-foot canal and dyke along the Steveston waterfront. (1908)(VPL)

The Years of Consolidation and Mechanization 1900 - 1919

Chapter 4

Main Channel of the Fraser River

The expansion of Roberts Bank continued until by 1905 the North Sand Heads Lighthouse stood one mile south of the main channel and the Black Buoy Channel was too shallow for shipping. The Department of Marine purchased, refurbished and anchored a schooner in the main channel in October 1905 to work in concert with the North Sand Heads Lighthouse. However, by 1911 the anchorage of the lightship had shallowed considerably with silting, and the ***SAND HEADS*** itself was leaking badly.

The Department purchased the ***THOMAS BAYARD***, a 94-foot schooner originally built in 1880 in New York as a pilot ship and refitted as a sealing schooner, to replace the ***SAND HEADS***. After seal hunting at sea was forbidden by a 1911 treaty between Great Britain, the United States, Russia and Japan, the ***BAYARD*** was converted to a lightship for Steveston and renamed ***SANDHEADS No. 16***. It watched over the boats entering the mouth of the Fraser River until 1956, and was eventually bought for the Vancouver Maritime Museum in 1978 and partially restored.

The Department of Marine initiated a programme in 1912 to control the flow of water at the mouth of the river by installing a system of jetties. The first section extended out approximately one mile from Garry Point and was completed in 1914. The second phase, completed between 1915 and 1917, extended out a further one and a half miles along Sturgeon Bank.

Town Site and Waterfront

After a severe flood in 1905 which set the wooden sidewalk on Second Avenue afloat, the Richmond municipality hired a floating dredge to dig a 33 foot canal and to build a new dyke around the island. Along much of the Steveston waterfront the ditch was dredged parallel and relatively close to the wood bulkhead dyke and boardwalk. However, the ditch and dyke were diverted inland around the Phoenix, Britannia and Pacific Coast Canneries because of the network of cannery houses and boardwalks built on pilings in this area around 1900.

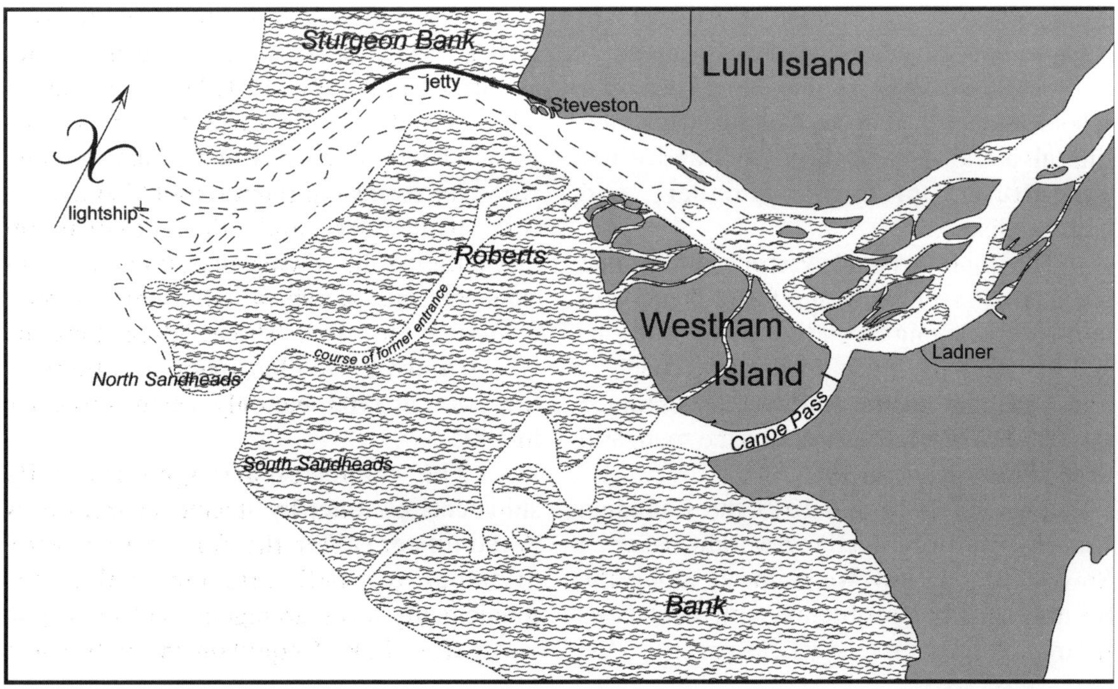

*Map of the Fraser River delta showing the channels of the South Arm, location of **SAND HEADS No.16** and the first two sections of the Steveston jetty. (Copied from Washington, Hydrographic Office, 1900, Chart 1768)*

The two-room Steveston Public School built in 1904. (ca. 1905)(HS)

The Canadian Pacific Railway completed its railroad tracks from Vancouver to Steveston in 1902, and operated trains powered by steam engines. The British Columbia Electric Railway began to use electric trams on the tracks in 1905. For the first time stores and homes in Steveston had electricity. The trams covered the fifteen-mile distance between Vancouver and Steveston in an hour, travelling at twenty miles per hour, but were capable of speeds of fifty miles per hour. Trams ran every hour during the day and every half hour morning and night for commuting cannery workers and other labourers. This service was dubbed the "Sockeye Special". The return fare between Vancouver and Steveston was eighty-five cents. Children paid nothing, but high school students had to pay full fare. This tram line also transported milk cans and other agricultural products, lumber and merchandise.

The improved road system and tram line made land travel easier and faster than water transport, bringing an end to the river ferries and replacing the horse-drawn stage coaches. The Canadian Pacific Railway discontinued the ***TRANSFER*** ferry service on the south arm of the Fraser River in 1908.

Between 1914 and 1917 the Canadian National Railway operated a train between Steveston and New Westminster along the South Arm, but problems with peat fires destroying tracks forced its closure.

After the railroad arrived in Steveston, lumber for the town could be hauled by rail from the new mills at Eburne (South Vancouver) to Tom Leslie's lumber yard. Sailing ships bound for Europe loaded lumber at the foot of Number One Road. With about fifteen canneries, a lumber dock and a new brick works, plus several more canneries directly across the river, Steveston was a major industrial destination on the lower mainland. Locals jokingly regarded Vancouver as an outport of Steveston.

While fresh water moorage cleared wooden-hulled ships of toredos, some clipper ships preferred to dock at Vancouver harbour, which was easier to navigate and had better facilities. For a while the federal government allowed sailing ships to be towed into the Fraser River's south arm to load salmon. However steamship interests lobbied against this procedure and the government discontinued the towing of sailing ships for safety reasons. Merchant sailing ships stopped coming to Steveston. Three sailing ships and six steamships loaded canned salmon at Steveston in 1903, but only steamships came in 1905.

The canneries arranged for daily shipments of water by steamboat from New Westminster. After the failure of several attempts to drill artesian wells, the municipality made arrangements to transport water from Lake Coquitlam in 1909, and a wooden water main to Steveston was completed in 1912.

The number of stores in Steveston had increased to forty-three by 1910. Twenty-four of these businesses were owned by Caucasians, ten by Japanese and eight by Chinese. Japanese stores were located along Moncton Street and Chinese shops on Number One Road south of Moncton Street. Steveston still only had twelve telephone subscribers.

Steveston Public School and Japanese School

Japanese parents wanted to give their children an education that would help them integrate into the Canadian community and assimilate back into the Japanese community if the family returned to their homeland. School-age children attended the Steveston School at Georgia Street and Second Avenue. By 1904 the one-room school house was too small and a new two-room school was built and painted green. The old school building was used for a playroom and storage area until it was torn down. Classes were integrated, with Lee Foo, Kiko Tamura, Fanny Phoenix and other unidentified Chinese, Japanese and Native children in class photographs from 1906 to 1909. In 1906 there were 35 children from 20 families in two classes from grade one to seven.

There were few Japanese children in Richmond at the turn of the century, but by 1907 they were the largest immigrant group. The Richmond School Board was formed in 1906. It ruled that only children whose parents owned property were eligible to attend public schools. This ruling effectively barred Japanese children from Steveston School, as most lived in houses owned by the canneries. In 1909 the Japanese community built their own four-room school south of the hospital on Number One Road. Japanese teachers were hired to teach the curriculum adopted from the Japanese school system. Nobutaro Takashima was the first principal. All children from the families living in cannery houses and some children from the families with property attended this school. Around 1914 Mrs. Chilton, wife of the Royal Bank manager, was hired by the Japanese community to teach English.

Early Fires

Fire was the principal hazard of pioneer settlements with wooden structures. The first major fire was an apparent arson early in the

The Japanese School on Number One Road, built in 1909 after the School Board barred children of non-propertied families from the Steveston Public School. (ca. 1910)(HS)

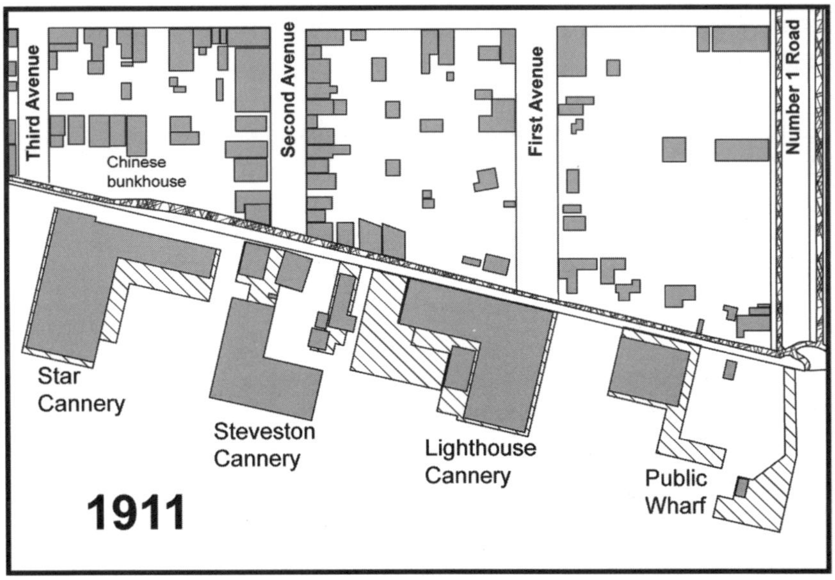

Map of part of the Steveston waterfront showing locations of canneries and Chinese living quarters. (BL)

morning on October 8, 1901. The fire caused damages assessed at $10,000, destroying a drug store, butcher shop, two barber shops, doctor's office, fruit stand and an unoccupied store.

A fire on the morning of April 5, 1907, consumed Steveston's China town along Number One Road. One hundred people were left homeless, mostly Chinese, some Japanese and three Caucasians. About fifteen buildings, owned mainly by Chinese merchants, were lost. These included stores, residences and houses of ill-repute, with an estimated value of $10,000. Four days later another fire started about three o'clock in the morning in the Lighthouse Cannery mess-house. A store and some cannery houses were demolished with damages of $4,000.

Eighteen months later on October 5, 1908, a fire razed the China town on Dyke Road between the Pacific Coast Cannery and the Hong Wo General Store. This fire caused $35,000 in damages, destroying four or five bunkhouses and several houses. Approximately 300 people were left homeless, of which half were Japanese.

By far the most disastrous fire in Steveston occurred on May 14, 1918. The fire reportedly started in the Star Cannery Chinese messhouse at approximately 8:30 am. It spread quickly, fanned by a high west wind. Fire Chief O'Neil and a small band of volunteers were on the scene soon after the first alarm, but their fire fighting attempts were frustrated by small hoses and weak water pressure. A frantic call for aid was answered by fire brigades from Vancouver and Point Grey. The Point Grey fire engine arrived shortly, and the large pump was hooked up to the water mains. Unfortunately, the Vancouver fire engine broke down about four miles from Steveston. The men in the brigade were able to commandeer private vehicles, and arrived in time to attach their hose to the centrifugal pump on the public works department boat 303. Their efforts helped save the recently built Columbia Cold Storage, and probably most of the canneries and associated buildings to the east. The fire burned itself out about noon, after destroying all buildings from the waterfront to Moncton Street, between Third Avenue and Number One Road. Only the brick Hepworth building on the southeast corner of Second Avenue was left standing. The Star, Steveston and Lighthouse Canneries were burnt down to the pilings. The heaviest losses were incurred by the Lighthouse Cannery where 22,000 cases of canned salmon were stored. The fire also eradicated three hotels (London, Richmond and Star), twenty small shops and about a hundred cannery houses. Many of the shops were owned by Japanese. An estimated six hundred Japanese and Chinese were left homeless by the fire. Japanese fishermen also lost twenty boats and one hundred nets which had been stored in the Star and Lighthouse Canneries. Many fishermen saved their nets by dragging them out of burning buildings and soaking them in the canals and ditches. Damages from this fire were assessed at $500,000.

Development of the Commercial Fishery

There were 3,683 Fraser River gillnet licenses in 1900, but only 1,396 licenses in 1911 and 1,337 licenses in 1919 (Appendix Table 2). Three reasons for this decline were interception by Puget Sound trap fisheries, the obstruction at Hell's Gate and possible over-fishing of off-year sockeye salmon runs. When boat engines were introduced in 1902, the more efficient gas-powered Columbia River boats also forced boats without power out of the fishery. After 1908 fishing was closed for 42 hours each week.

Catches from the dominant year runs reached 27.6 million in 1901, 21.9 million in

A view of cannery row from the Columbia Cold Storage building, showing charred pilings of the Lighthouse, Steveston and Star Canneries after the fire of 1918, with the Gulf of Georgia Cannery in the background. (1918) (CRA)

1905, and 23.1 million in 1909 (Appendix Table 1). However, catches from the off-year runs to 1912 averaged only 3.8 million fish per year, down from an average of 4.8 million during the 1890s. Scientists attributed this decline to increased fishing effort in both countries after 1895 and to a dam at Quesnel Lake. The American fishtrap and purse seine fisheries caught 60 percent of the Fraser River sockeye salmon between 1900 and 1919.

In 1911 the Canadian Northern Railway, later known as the Canadian National Railway, started construction of a rail line on the east bank of the Fraser River between Yale and

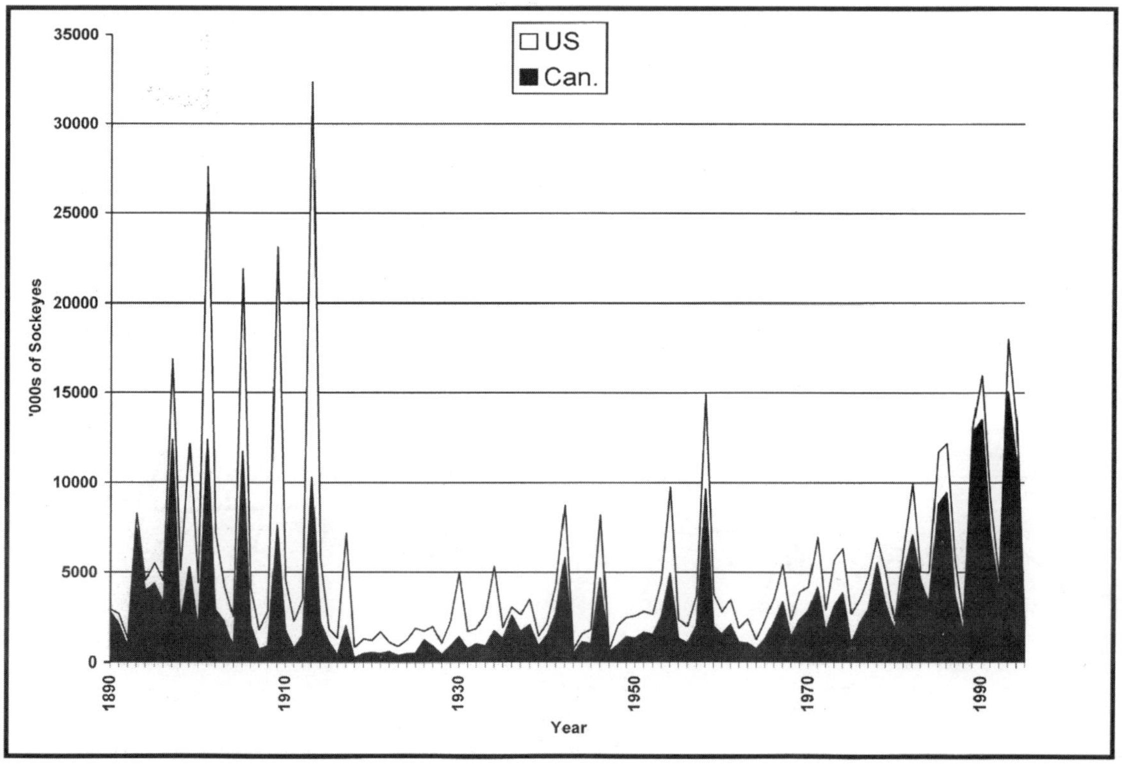

Landing of Fraser River sockeye salmon by country, 1890 - 1995. (source - Pacific Salmon Commission)

Lytton. Workers dumped large quantities of rock into the river in 1912, and changed the flow pattern of the river. The effects of this first became apparent in July 1913, when a massive build-up of sockeye perished at Hell's Gate, unable to continue their journey upriver to spawn. On February 23, 1914, a large rock slide on the east bank of Hell's Gate increased the devastation.

The sockeye catch for the dominant year runs plummeted from 32.3 million fish in 1913 to 7.2 million in 1917 and l.7 million in 1921. Catches for the off-year runs from 1914 to 1919 further declined to an average of 2.2 million fish per year.

Canneries and Other Waterfront Enterprises

The unbridled optimism of the 1890s, which fuelled the rapid growth in the number of canneries on the Steveston waterfront, was replaced by dire pessimism for the salmon canning industry in the 1900s. People were starting to realize that salmon was not an inexhaustible resource. The expanding trap fishery in Puget Sound developed rapidly during the 1890s, taking a larger percentage of the Fraser River sockeye catch. The obstruction of Hell's Gate gorge in 1912 prevented Fraser River salmon from spawning. The salmon runs of the Columbia River also

Map of the Steveston waterfront showing locations of canneries in 1911. (solid buildings - operating: clear building - not operating)

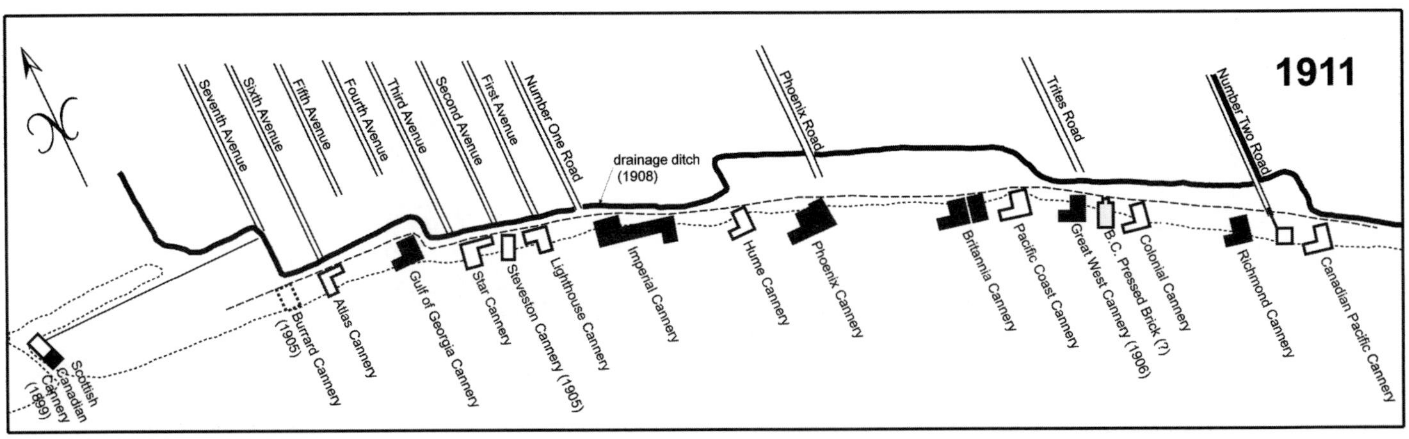

Cannery row from the Gulf of Georgia Cannery to the Canadian Pacific Cannery. These three photographs were found over the window in the wheelhouse of the pilot boat. (ca. 1908)(HS)

showed signs of overfishing, providing additional evidence that these resources were finitc.

Another reason for gloom was the glut of canned salmon resulting from the profusion of canneries in British Columbia, Puget Sound and Alaska in the 1890s. The world-wide output of canned salmon reached 5.2 million cases in 1901. Prices for canned salmon fell to historic lows while production costs rose.

The largest fisheries merger on this coast was negotiated in 1902, when the British Columbia Packers Association (BC Packers) purchased the assets of thirty-five canneries. This association hoped to increase profits by reducing competition for fish and seasonal labour, and by concentrating production facilities in a few strategic locations. Included in this amalgamation were eight canneries on the Steveston waterfront (Canadian Pacific, Colonial, Pacific Coast, Hume, Imperial, Brunswick #1, London and Atlas Canneries) under superintendent Ninian H. Bain.

Fifteen canneries on the Steveston waterfront were operating in 1900. Three new canneries were added in 1905 and 1906, but only six Steveston canneries operated in 1911 (Imperial, Britannia, Phoenix, Gulf of Georgia, Richmond, and Great West).

Steveston Cannery (1905)

The Steveston Canning Company built their second cannery on the site of the City Wharf at the foot of Second Avenue. The fire

The Imperial Cannery (right) enlarged by the British Columbia Packers Association in 1903, and the Brunswick Cannery (left) converted into a warehouse. (1908) (VPL)

Cannery row: from the left, the Burrard Cannery (?), the Gulf of Georgia Cannery, the Star Cannery, the Garry Point lighthouse, and the Imperial Cannery. (1908)(VPL)

insurance map for 1911 showed a long building on an enlarged wharf. This cannery was closed down after 1907, and was destroyed by the 1918 fire.

Burrard Cannery (1905)

Little is known about this cannery. It was built by the Burrard Canning Company near the foot of Seventh Avenue, and was reportedly destroyed by fire in 1910. The fire insurance map for 1911 showed a small warehouse inside the dike and a narrow T-shaped wharf with a small gutting shed outside the dike at the foot of Seventh Avenue. A large building photographed there by Philip Timms in 1908 was probably the Burrard Cannery.

Great West Cannery (1906)

This cannery was built between the Pacific Coast Cannery and Colonial Cannery by George Alexander's Great West Packing Company. It was commonly called the "Alexander Cannery" by the Japanese. This small plant with one canning line operated for 51 years, making it the third longest operating cannery on the Steveston waterfront. It was demolished by fire on October 15, 1961. Nelson Brothers Fisheries Company purchased the property and erected an ice plant on this site. The entire Nelson Brothers Fisheries complex was taken over in 1968 by British Columbia Packers Ltd.

The British Columbia Pressed Brick Company which operated from about 1900 to the 1930s. (1908)(VPL)

British Columbia Pressed Brick Company

Little is known of this company. It was established immediately west of the Colonial Cannery in the early 1900s and operated until some time in the 1930s. This site was taken over by the Nelson Brothers Fisheries Company and used for some time to render herring into fish meal and oil. The building became the machine shop of Trites Marine Services Ltd.

Columbia Cold Storage (1915)

BC Packers purchased the London Cannery in 1902, and the building was torn down soon after. The Columbia Cold Storage was constructed on the site in 1915, and was demolished some time before 1946.

Canning Operations

Two machines greatly automated the salmon canning operation. The first of these was the butchering machine, named the "Iron Chink" because it replaced large crews of Chinese butchers. It was introduced in 1903 by the E.A. Smith Cannery Machines Company of Seattle. This was the only machine developed exclusively for the salmon canning industry. All of the other innovations

The interior of a cannery with its Smith butchering machine in the foreground. (ca. 1910)(CVA)

were adapted from the vegetable and meat processing industries. The butchering process had required a gang of eighteen to thirty men to butcher enough salmon to supply a canning line. The Smith butchering machine, operated by three men, could process between 60 and 75 fish per minute, greatly lowering labour costs and increasing the efficiency of the canning operation. The machine cut off each salmon's fins and head, and gutted the carcass. It reduced waste by butchering fish very uniformly. It also required much less space than the manual system, thereby freeing cannery floor space for more canning lines or storage.

The solderless can-making machine was introduced in 1912. This machine crimped the cylindrical side and bottom of the can with a lock and lap seam, thus sealing the joint without solder. It eliminated the need for a large can-making crew, and decreased the number of faulty canned products. It also reduced the risk of running out of cans and having to stop canning for the season. The Automatic Can Company in New Westminster, under superintendent Henry Schaake, could manufacture 200,000 machine-made cans for salmon, fruit and vegetables each day.

The arrival of electricity at Steveston in 1905 supplied another source of light and power to the canneries on the Steveston waterfront, but the steam engine still provided power for most of the machines. The materials were moved by conveyors, and the machines were powered by a system of shafts, pulleys and belts. The Smith butchering machine and the solderless can-making machine reduced the number of men needed to crew a canning line. Between 120 and 140 men were required in 1893, but only 84 men in 1905. Thus BC Packers was able to upgrade the Imperial Cannery to four canning lines.

Before 1900 the industrial centre of the province was Victoria. Many of the machines and pieces of equipment used by canneries were made by the Albion Iron Works. After 1900 Letson and Burpee of Vancouver and Schaake of New Westminster were the principal manufacturers of canning machines such as filling machines, fish elevators, powered gang knives, retorts, hand trucks, coolers and trays.

Henry Doyle left the following description of salmon canning in the first decade of the Twentieth Century. Fish were lifted by elevators from scows into the cannery,

Japanese women filling cans with salmon pieces. Many women have babies strapped on their backs. (1908)(VPL)

and sorted by species. Those slated for canning were passed through the "Iron Chink", which chopped off the heads, tails and body fins, slit open the bellies, and removed the guts. Workers called slimers scraped the body cavities clean, dropped the fish into a tank of fresh water, and examined them for remains of entrails and blood clots.

After cleaning, fish were soaked in a strong brine solution for about twenty minutes to give them a salty flavour. Brining was preferred to adding salt to each can, because brine removed some of the slime, resulting in a cleaner product. After draining, they were taken to the gang knife to be cut into can-sized steaks.

The fish pieces were conveyed to the fillers who put the pieces into cans. A can-filling machine was invented about 1912. This machine used a plunger to fill 75 to 100 cans

The Atagi Boat Works with a newly constructed packer boat and a seine boat on the ways ready for launching. (ca. 1920)(Atagi Family collection)

each minute. However, Fraser River canneries seldom used these machines to process sockeye salmon because the canned product was inferior. The filled cans were carried on another conveyer belt to the weighing machine, which rejected light cans. The cans were then passed to the clincher, a machine that attached the tops firmly on the can, but not air tight.

After the cans were topped, they were moved to the steam box and heated to 200 degrees Fahrenheit for about fourteen minutes to expel the air from the cans and create a vacuum. They were then passed to the closing machine which hermetically sealed the cans.

The cans were cleaned in washing tanks, and packed into woven metal coolers, which were stacked onto hand trucks on rails. When enough trucks were loaded, they were rolled into the retort, the doors were closed and steam was turned on. The cans were cooked for 75 minutes at a steam pressure of fifteen pounds and a temperature between 238 and 242 degrees Fahrenheit.

After cooking the coolers were removed from the hand trucks, rinsed in clean water, stacked and left to cool. The cans were then taken to the lacquering machine where they were coated with a thin layer of lacquer to prevent rusting. Finally the cans were labelled and boxed for shipment.

Cannery Workers

As mechanization of the canning line increased, more Caucasian men were needed to fill the supervisory positions in the cannery, while the numbers of Chinese workers decreased substantially. By 1901 about eight percent of British Columbia's population was Chinese. The federal government increased the head tax for each immigrant from $50 to $100 in 1900, and to $500 in 1904 under the Federal Chinese Immigration Act of Canada..

Most Native families stopped travelling to Steveston for the fishing season when the tasks completed by Native women in the canneries were taken over by the recently arrived wives of Japanese fishermen.

Boat Works

In the early 1900s Japanese boat builders dominated the small boat building industry.

The Phoenix Cannery with grounded Columbia River type boats, powered gillnetters and a fish scow, with ways for K. Kishi Boat Works in the foreground. (ca. 1915)(CRA)

The Vancouver Ship's Registry listed two Steveston boat works in 1904. From 1904 to 1919, nineteen different Japanese boat works were listed in the Ship's Registry. This list included only those boats examined by a marine surveyor, and excluded most of the small fishing boats built by the Japanese boat works. Several large boat works built small gillnetters as well as larger seine boats and packers.

George Isomura operated an independent boat works in Steveston from 1903 to about 1912. Atagi Boat Works was started by T. Atagi in 1905 beside the boardwalk to the Scottish Canadian Cannery. This boat works built all but one of the ***QUATHIASKI*** fleet of seine boats. In 1907 the Tanaka and Nakade Boat Works was sited between Fifth and Sixth Avenues on Chatham Street. Another boat works was started by the Kishi Brothers west of the Phoenix Cannery about 1914.

Fishing Boats

Gasoline engines were first used in the Fraser River gillnet fishery about 1902. One of the first gillnet vessels to be motorized was a 25-foot dugout canoe belonging to a fisherman from Barnston Island, which was fitted by Easthope and Sons with a 5-horsepower engine. A Columbia River boat or Bristol Bay boat was motorized by replacing the centre board with a gasoline engine, and boring a hole through the skeg for the propeller shaft. A small wooden cabin was added over the forward end of the vessel to protect the engine and provide shelter for the fisherman. Originally the single level cabin had a sliding top and side door. The fish hold immediately

A Columbia River type boat powered with a gasoline engine. (ca. 1915)(MY)

aft of the cabin was covered with cedar planks. The net storage and work well occupied about one-third of the vessel's length.

Fishermen quickly realized the advantages of a powered vessel and began to install engines into their gillnetters. A gas-powered vessel had greater control over wind and current, was faster and more maneuverable, and required less crew than a sail-powered vessel. The pictures of the Steveston waterfront taken by Philip Timms in 1908 showed only Columbia River boats rigged with masts, but the pictures by F. Dundas Todd in 1913 showed many boats with cabins and no masts. The original two-cycle engines were soon replaced by four-cycle units which were more fuel efficient and did not vibrate as much. Gasoline engines used to motorize the Fraser River gillnet fleet included Easthope (Vancouver), Vivian (Vancouver), Letson and Burpee (Vancouver) and Cowie (Vancouver). The Cowie engine was also manufactured under license by the Schaake Machine Works, Limited (New Westminster).

Easthope and Sons began making two-cycle engines and installing them in the Columbia River boats of independent fishermen at their new facilities in Coal Harbour around 1905. Their four-cycle Heavy Duty Marine Engine, introduced about 1917, was popular with fishermen because of its low cost, simplicity and reliability. Easthope kept costs low by using parts mass-produced by other companies such as Model T pistons and valves made by the Ford Motor Company. An Easthope engine was fitted with a dual ignition system consisting of a timer with a dry cell battery and a magneto. Batteries were notoriously unreliable and this feature gave fishermen a back-up system to start the engine. Castings for the Easthope engines were made heavier for greater durability. These engines were simply and strongly constructed, with easy access to all parts so that repairs could

Columbia River type boats tied to the Steveston Cannery wharf, with the Lighthouse Cannery in the background. (ca. 1910)(HS)

Tom Howard, Ed Ireland and an unidentified person inside the marine blacksmith section of the Cory, Cole and Howard shop on Number One Road. The net guards are ready for installing around the propeller of a gillnetter. (ca. 1913) (HS)

be made by people with little knowledge of engines. The Easthope family operated a shop on Number One Road in Steveston from 1930 to 1987.

Net rollers were first used in the early 1900s. Each detachable unit consisted of a large horizontal roller and two smaller vertical rollers. The fisherman set the rollers in the mount on the stern, and hauled in the net. Then he detached the rollers from the mount, and stored them in the net well or on the fish hatch. At first he set the net by dragging it out over the stern without the rollers as the boat moved forward.

Soon after engines were added to the Columbia River boats, net guards were developed by Ed Ireland, a blacksmith by trade and an inveterate inventor by nature. He developed blacksmithing tools, apple-picking machines, and many other creations. He was also an amateur magician, frequently demonstrating sleight-of-hand tricks to an appreciative crowd.

Wharves

Both Columbia River boats and engine-powered boats were moored perpendicular to the wharf to accommodate the increased number of fishing vessels. One end of each vessel was tied to the wharf and the other to an anchor or a piling of the protection boom. Even the gas-powered boats were light enough to beach beside the canneries.

As more fishermen became independent, canneries had to provide better services to retain them. The wharves for net racks began to be completely decked during this period.

Fishermen

After the limit on the number of licenses was abolished, the canning companies encouraged fishermen to own their own boats and nets. This transferred an ever increasing financial burden onto the fishermen. Companies loaned money for fishing boats and equipment to Japanese immigrants who sold fish to them. Japanese fishermen were also bound to the companies for housing and storage facilities and equipment maintenance. In addition, the companies gave advances to cover living expenses during the fishing season. In the early 1900s most Japanese fishermen owned only their fishing licenses, and were entirely dependent on the canneries.

Strikes in 1900 and 1901

Companies were being squeezed by rising operating costs and intense competition, especially from American canneries in Puget Sound with access to low-cost fish caught in traps. When license limits were abolished, fishermen also had to contend with higher

Japanese fisherman mending a gillnet hung on a net rack, with bluestone tanks on the right. Net wharves were completely planked after the turn of the century. (1908) (VPL)

operating costs and increased competition. Of the 3,683 licenses issued for the Fraser River in 1900, 555 (15%) were to Natives, 1,076 (29%) to Caucasians, 1,659 (45%) to Japanese and 393 (11%) to companies. Japanese also fished most of the company licenses.

As the numbers of canneries and fishermen increased, harsh economic conditions fuelled by racial conflicts exploded into the most violent strikes in the salmon fishing industry.

The companies offered the fishermen fifteen cents per fish in 1900, five cents less than the previous year. They were united under the Fraser River Canners' Association with spokesman Henry Bell-Irving. The fishermen demanded twenty-five cents per fish. They were represented by three separate organizations: the Natives by tribal groups, the Caucasians by the newly formed BC Fishermen's Union and the Japanese by the Fishermen's Benevolent Society.

The strike started on July 8 and continued with minor incidents for almost two weeks. On July 22 the companies offered twenty cents per fish for the first 600 and fifteen cents per

Militia camped in front of the Gulf of Georgia Cannery. (1900)(VPL)

fish above this number. Japanese fishermen met the following day, and decided to accept this offer. For most Japanese, fishing was their only means of livelihood. Also, threats of eviction from cannery houses were especially frightening to the Japanese. Natives and most Caucasians had permanent residences, and could more readily find work in other industries.

Citing the threat of violence on the fishing grounds, the Fraser River Canners' Association petitioned three local Justices of the Peace to declare Martial Law, ostensibly to maintain order. A few minutes before midnight of July 23, Colonel Worsnop of the 6th Duke of Connaught's Own Rifles in Vancouver received the declaration of Martial Law and sent the bugler to muster the troops. About 100 officers and men assembled at the Union Steamship wharf and embarked on the ***SS COMOX***. They arrived in Steveston early on July 24 and were soon joined by an additional fifty men aboard the ***SS RITHET*** from New Westminster. The troops pitched their tents besides the Gulf of Georgia Cannery and were stationed at the Phoenix, Gulf of Georgia and Scottish Canadian Canneries.

The Japanese started fishing that morning, but the Native and Caucasian fishermen clung to their demands for higher prices. The strikers were supported by the Native women who refused to work on the sliming and filling lines. The canneries could not operate without these women. The Union and the Association resumed negotiations, and finally on July 30 they agreed on a price of nineteen cents per fish for the entire season. All of the fishermen were out on the fishing grounds the following day.

Anticipating a big sockeye salmon run in 1901, the canneries lowered the price again to twelve and a half cents per fish caught before July 27, and ten cents for the remainder of the season. The fishermen demanded fifteen cents for the entire season, and went on strike June 30. The fishing fleet remained idle during the first week of the strike even though the Japanese had agreed to a price of twelve and a

Columbia River type boats and gasoline engine-powered boats at moorage along a wharf, with boat works ways in the foreground and Lighthouse Cannery in the background. (1913) (VPL)

Plan of Scottish Canadian Cannery complex in 1923. (IAO)

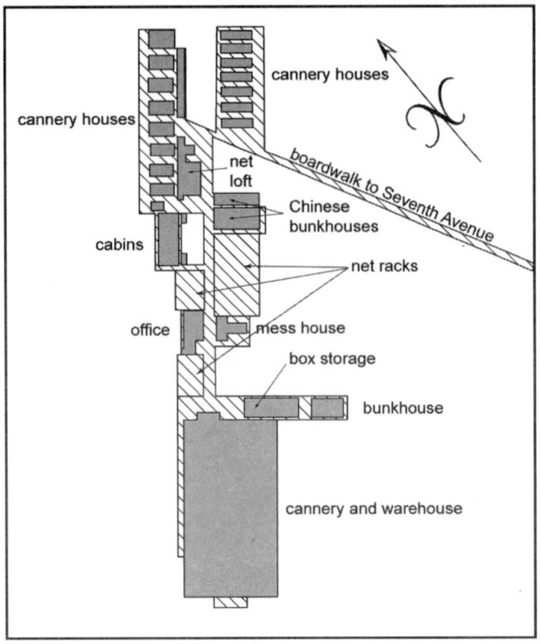

half cents until August 3 and a 250-fish limit after this date. However, by the second week, a few Japanese started fishing and soon were joined by hundreds of others. There were reports of fishermen being beaten up, net slashings and boats set adrift. One group of Japanese fishermen were found marooned on Bowen Island. On July 19 the fishermen ended the strike by agreeing to twelve and a half cents for the first quarter of the pack and ten cents for the remainder.

Japanese Immigration

Before 1908 there were no restrictions on Japanese immigration into Canada. The number of Japanese immigrants increased from 354 in 1904/1905 to 7,601 in 1907/1908. Of these, 6,945 were males and 566 were females. Natives and Caucasians, fearing complete domination of the fishing industry by the Japanese, demanded stricter controls. One of the Liberal Party slogans in the 1908 federal election was "White Fishermen Only!"

Under the Lemieux agreement negotiated by the federal government in 1908, Japan voluntarily limited the number of male immigrants to 400 per year. Because the agreement did not limit women and children, it encouraged married men to send for their wives, and unmarried men to find mates by the 'picture bride' scheme. A single male would inform his relatives in Japan that he was ready to be married. They would canvass the village for a suitable wife and make an agreement with her parents. They would send

Cannery houses for Japanese families on the Scottish Canadian Cannery premises and Columbia River type boats moored in the Scotch slough. (ca. 1903)(HS)

photographs, and if the prospective groom liked what he saw, he would inform his relatives, and a "marriage" would be registered in Japan. The husband and wife would then exchange letters, and the husband would arrange for a passport and passage for his wife.

The arrival of wives changed the priorities of Japanese immigrants from saving as much as possible for a future life in Japan to trying to improve their conditions in Canada. One of their priorities was suitable homes for their families. The companies were eager to retain fishermen, guarantee future supplies of fish and attract diligent cannery workers. By 1911 single family cannery houses had appeared around all the canneries. The increase in Japanese families changed Steveston from a "boom and bust" settlement to one with a stable, moderate population. Japanese families settled permanently in the houses furnished by the canneries. In exchange for low-rent housing, the men sold their catches to the cannery and the women worked on its canning lines.

Canneries were generally operated from June to the middle of September. After the canneries were shut down for the season,

A Japanese 'picture bride' on board a steamship en route to a new life. (ca. 1905) (UBC-SC)

Japanese workers turning salted chum salmon on the Gulf of Georgia premises with the Star Cannery in the background. (1908)(VPL)

Japanese Imperial Navy training vessels off Steveston surrounded by a flotilla of gillnetters bidding farewell. A rare instance of 'Sutebusuton' (meaning Steveston) spelled with Chinese characters. (1914) (JCNM)

A decorated fish packer boat with a deckload of Steveston residents honouring the official visit of the Japanese Imperial Navy. (1914) (HS)

Japanese fishermen continued until late fall to fish for chum salmon, which were salted for export to Japan. Each fisherman also salted enough chum salmon in wooden boxes to last his family through the winter. Rice and salted chum salmon were their staple winter foods.

After the fishing season the men would leave Steveston to find work either in the herring salteries of the Gulf Islands or in lumber camps. A few fishermen would jig for lingcod, and others would troll for bluebacks (small coho salmon) in the Gulf Islands. However, their families remained in Steveston. After the canning season the women found occasional work picking berries and harvesting crops on the neighbouring truck farms, and the children attended kindergarten and school.

Thirty years after the first Japanese fishermen arrived in Steveston, a few Japanese owned businesses and properties, but most owned only their fishing licenses and mortgaged boats. The majority spoke only Japanese. They had retained the Japanese cultural, social and political values, and their ties with Japan. Their sole concession to the Canadian way of life was the universal adoption of western clothes, which were more practical and more readily available than Japanese clothes.

The Japanese enthusiastically celebrated the arrival of all Japanese emissaries to the British Columbia coast. A flotilla of Steveston fishing boats steamed out to the mouth of the Fraser River to bid farewell to the Japanese Navy warships ***ASAMA*** and ***AZUMA*** after an official visit to Vancouver in June 1914. Warships from the Japanese Navy patrolled the west coast of Canada during World War I, while British Admiralty warships were deployed in more strategic areas.

By 1919 only 1,337 fishermen held fishing licenses on the Fraser River. Of these, 65% were Japanese, 22% were Caucasian and 4% were Native (Appendix Table 2). Native and Caucasian fishermen left the decimated Fraser River for other more lucrative fisheries and occupations. For example, Ed Sparrow, a Native leader, fished for sockeye salmon on the Fraser River from 1909 to 1916, then switched to fishing the Skeena River from 1924 to 1942. He also gillnetted the Fraser River in the fall after the Skeena River season. Japanese fishermen with Fraser River gillnetting licenses were not allowed to fish in other districts.

The Years of Uncertainty

Chapter 5

1920-1939

Main Channel of the Fraser River

Silting kept shifting the course of the main navigation channel of the Fraser River. In 1914 the Department of Public Works initiated a jetty construction programme to control the course of the main channel. The North Jetty was constructed in six phases from 1914 to 1932. This jetty extended out approximately 5 miles from off Garry Point to the ***SAND HEADS No. 16*** lightship. The North Jetty and Wingdams #1, #2 and #3 were placed on the north side of the main channel. The Woodward Training Wall, South Jetty, Albion Dyke and Albion Dyke #1 were constructed on the south side of the main channel. The jetties built in the 1920s, as well as the Albion Dyke and Albion Dyke #1, were walls of double pilings. Conversely, the South Jetty, the eastern extension of the Woodward Training Wall and the repairs to the North Jetty started in the 1930s were walls of boulders.

Townsite and Waterfront

By 1920 Steveston had grown into a bustling coastal village, thriving on the salmon fishing industry, and to a lesser extent on small businesses and truck farming. Wrigley's British Columbia Directory for 1920 showed seventeen Japanese-owned businesses in Steveston and fourteen owned by Caucasians. Ten years later there were thirty-one Japanese and twenty-four Caucasian businesses.

Fire struck the Steveston waterfront again. On May 11, 1924, a fire was apparently started by an overheated stovepipe in a cannery house occupied by the Yesaki family at the Richmond Cannery. Two occupants raised the alarm, but the fire soon engulfed two other cannery houses and raged out of control, fanned by a southwest wind. The fire destroyed the Canadian Pacific and Richmond Canneries, two wharves, forty houses and eight gillnetters. Three hundred Japanese residents were left homeless. Damage was estimated at $150,000. Much of this loss was incurred by the

*The Canadian Pacific Railway docking ramp for the **MOTOR PRINCESS** at the foot of the alley between Sixth and Seventh Avenues. (ca. 1945)(HS)*

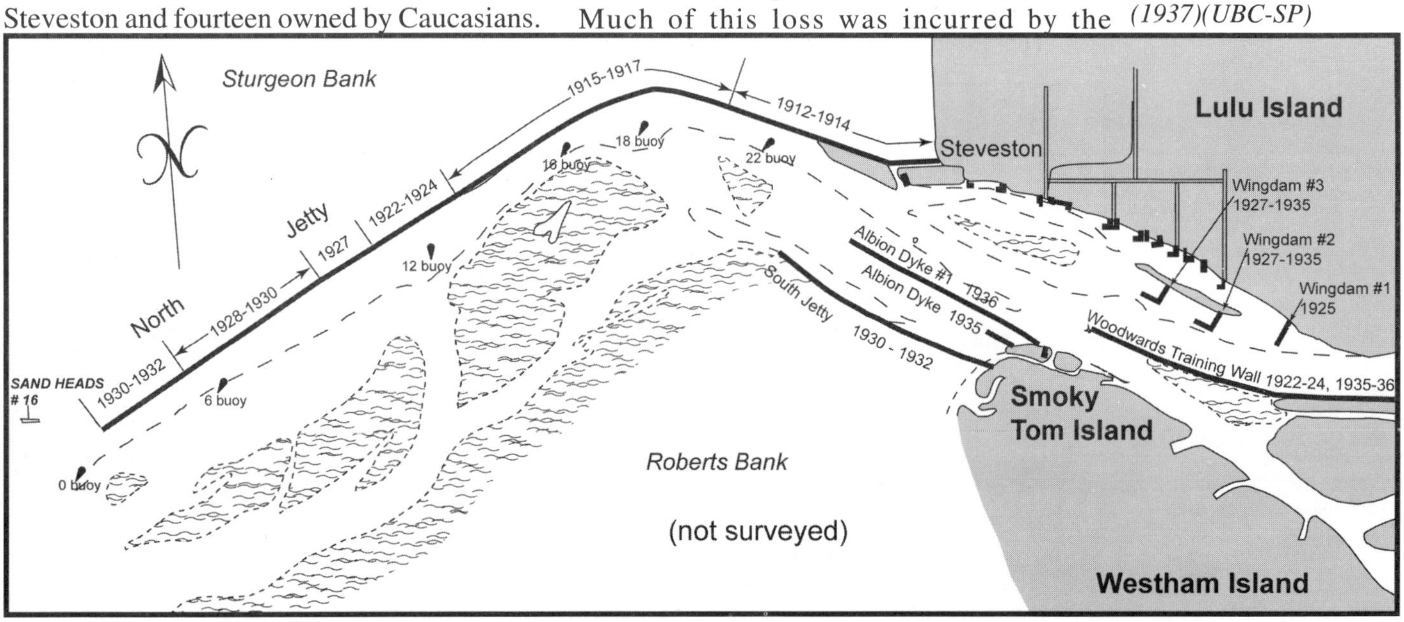

Map of the main Channel of the Fraser River showing the jetties constructed to control the flow of the river. (1937)(UBC-SP)

The ferry ***MOTOR PRINCESS****, operated by the Canadian Pacific Railway between Steveston and Sydney from 1929 to 1950. (ca. 1945)(HS)*

Richmond Cannery, which had 4,000 cases of canned salmon in storage.

The Canadian Pacific Railway started a daily ferry service with the ***MOTOR PRINCESS*** between Steveston and Sydney in 1929. This vessel initially carried 45 vehicles, but as automobiles increased in size, its capacity was reduced to 40 vehicles. This ferry docked at a ramp constructed from a railway turntable at the foot of Ferry Road between Sixth and Seventh Avenues.

Lord Byng School

The Japanese community continued to lobby for an integrated school system. Richmond began building a new four-room school in 1921 beside Steveston Public School. In 1922, when half of it was completed, it was renamed the Lord Byng School to honour the governor-general of Canada. In 1923 the Richmond School Board finally agreed to provide the necessary teachers, and take responsibility for teaching Japanese children. With this commitment the Japanese community raised the money to finish the school in 1925, providing four classrooms with a full basement. By 1928 this new school was already too small, and eight classes of 40 to 45 students were being held in various annexes, including the Japanese School. Jessie Steves (Hall), Elsie Esplin (Hunter), and Elva Carson (Moorside) all taught at the Japanese school. Hideko Hyodo (Shimuzu), one of two Japanese to obtain a British Columbia teaching certificate before the Second World War, was a member of the Steveston Public School staff.

The Japanese community leaders submitted a proposal to the provincial government. They offered to contribute one-half the cost of a larger school, if they could teach Japanese language classes there after regular classes. This proposal was accepted, and in 1930 a new 14-room two-storey school was constructed with $20,000 from the provincial government and $20,000 from the Japanese community. The Richmond School Board provided $8,000 for furnishings.

Japanese Kindergarten

In 1925 Marpole School, Simon Fraser

The fourteen-room Lord Byng School built in 1930 with financial contributions from the Japanese community. (ca. 1935)(HS)

School and Henry Hudson School in Vancouver began segregating Oriental children to avoid the extra cost of special classes to teach them English. Fearing segregation of Lord Byng because many Japanese children were not conversant in English, the Japanese Fishermen's Benevolent Society asked the Women's Missionary Society of the United Church (a 1925 union of Methodists, Presbyterians and Baptists) to start a kindergarten. The kindergarten opened in September 1925 with an enrolment of 55 students. It was so successful that an afternoon class was started in February 1926. A total of 121 children were enrolled in the first year.

The building used for the kindergarten classes soon became too small. The Japanese Women's Association (Fujinkai) started a fund-raising campaign in 1927 and collected $3,000 to build a larger kindergarten. A two-story building on Chatham Street, furnished with modern equipment, was completed in 1928. The Fujinkai paid for utilities, maintenance and a portion of the janitor's salary, and the Women's Missionary Society provided the teachers. Among the early teachers were Miss Lane, Miss Cotton and Miss Barry.

The success of the kindergarten prompted the Fujinkai in 1935 to start a day nursery for pre-kindergarten children during the six-month fishing season. The well-attended monthly mother's meeting was the chief social event for most of the mothers. Another popular monthly event initiated by the Methodist Church, continued by the United Church, and eventually taken over by the Fujinkai, was the cooking class.

The Franciscan Sisters of the Atonement (Roman Catholic Church) began their missionary work with the Steveston Japanese in 1931. They ran a day nursery for Japanese children from 7 am to 6 pm, charging ten cents per day or fifteen cents for bottle babies. In 1935 they also opened a kindergarten in the same building at the northwest corner of Richmond Street and Second Avenue. This building was moved to the Britannia Heritage

The graduating class of 1935 in front of the Japanese kindergarten operated by the Japanese Women's Association (Fujinkai) and staffed bt the Women's Missionary Society of the United Church. (1935)(MY)

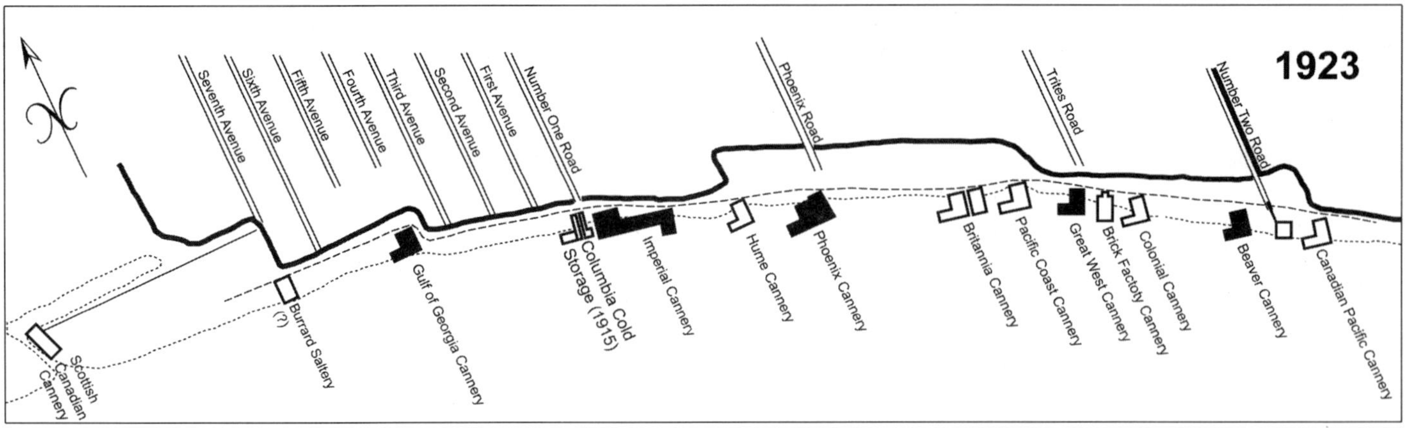

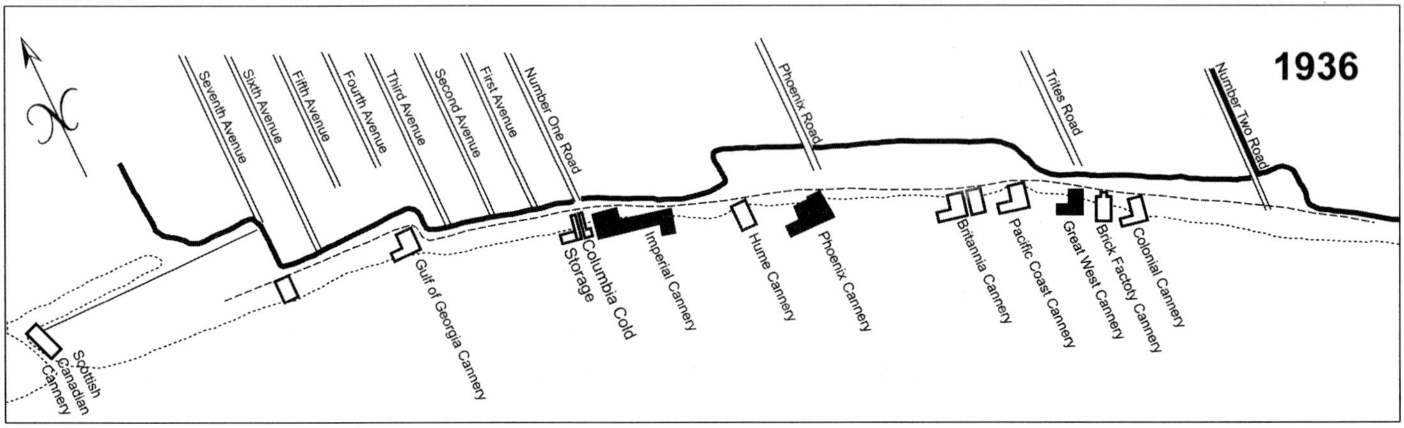

Maps of Steveston waterfront showing locations of canneries in 1923 and 1936 (solid buildings - operating; clear - not operating) (IAO)(CR)

Shipyard site in 1993.

Most of the Japanese women worked in the canneries and on the nearby berry and vegetable farms. They really appreciated the kindergartens and day nurseries which provided safe places for their children while they were at work, and introduced the children to the English language.

Buddhist Temple

Unlike Buddhists, Christians have a long history of missionary work in domestic and foreign countries, and the Japanese Methodists from United States had established a mission for Japanese fishermen in Steveston by 1895, and a church by 1910. Most of the Japanese remained Buddhists, but there was no Buddhist temple until 1928 for several reasons. First, during the early years fishermen were interested primarily in earning a living. Second, the fishermen were concerned that a foreign religion would aggravate anti-Japanese sentiments. A third reason was the lack of a Buddhist missionary tradition, possibly because of Japan's long isolation imposed by the Tokugawa Shogunate. The Buddhist temple was eventually built in Steveston on the west side of First Avenue between Moncton Street and the dyke. This building became the Steva theatre in 1946, and later held commercial businesses.

Development of the Commercial Fishery

The governments of Canada and United States had agreed before 1913 that they needed a single agency to manage the Fraser River

Miyakichi Yesaki's gillnetter built by S. Kishi's Richmond Boat Works in 1937, and powered by an 8-12 HP Easthope engine. From the right, the buildings in the background are Great West Cannery, its office, four cannery houses, a Chinese bunkhouse, a residence and the Hong Wo complex. (1938)(MY)

fishery effectively. Negotiations resulted in treaty proposals in 1909 and 1919, which the United States government refused to ratify. Eventually a new treaty stipulating equal division of catch was signed in Washington DC in May 1930. This treaty was modified and finally approved by all levels of the United States government in July 1937, setting a mandate for the protection, preservation and extension of the sockeye salmon fishery of the Fraser River. However, the International Pacific Salmon Fisheries Commission established by this treaty could not propose or enforce regulations until it had conducted eight years of scientific investigations.

The devastation caused by the Hell's Gate obstruction continued through this period. The catches of Fraser River sockeye decreased from an average of 3.1 million sockeye per year during 1914 - 1919 to 1.5 million per year during 1920 - 1929, with no clearly dominant years. The American share during the 1920s was 57 percent.

Recovery was evident during the 1930s as 1930, 1934, and 1938 emerged as dominant-cycle years with an average of 4.6 million sockeye, while the off-cycle years averaged 2.0 million. Canadians got only 35 percent of the Fraser River sockeye catch between 1930 and 1934. However, this share increased to 64 percent between 1935 and 1939, because Canadian fishermen fishing Johnstone Straits made exceptional catches of Fraser River sockeye salmon in 1936. The number of fishing days remained at 5.0 days per week.

Canneries and Other Waterfront Enterprises

No new canneries were built during this period on the Steveston waterfront. Five canneries operated in 1923. The Richmond Cannery burned in 1924.

The New England Fish Company had been active in the British Columbia halibut industry since 1893, and had operated under the name Canadian Fishing Company (CanFisCo) since 1906. In 1918 CanFisCo established its first salmon cannery, the Home Cannery in Vancouver, and by 1926 it had purchased 12 other canneries in British Columbia, including the Gulf of Georgia Cannery in Steveston. Because of this

Cannery row: from the left, the Burrard saltery, the Columbia Cold Storage, the Imperial Cannery (gray) and the Phoenix Cannery (white). The powered gillnetters moored perpendicular to wharf have various styles and sizes of cabins. (ca. 1930)(HS)

The only original 'Native hut" remaining on the Steveston waterfront. The building was converted into a gillnet shed sometime after the turn of the century.(1971)(MY)

consolidation, the Gulf of Georgia Cannery ceased canning salmon in 1930.

In 1925 Henry Doyle proposed another amalgamation of 61 salmon canneries by BC Packers in British Columbia. The average value of these canneries was $113,800, over three times the average value of the 39 canneries included in the proposed amalgamation drafted in 1901. BC Packers closed their can-making plant at the Imperial Cannery in 1927, and turned to the American Can Company to supply all their cans. In 1928 BC Packers amalgamated with Gosse Packing Company and Millerd Packing Company. This association now owned 44 canneries, 3 cold storages, 2 salteries and 5 fishmeal plants in British Columbia. In 1930 BC Packers canned 46.8 percent of the total British Columbia pack of 2,221,819 cases, but still lost $1,266,000 as sales plummeted because of the American stock market crash and resulting Depression. BC Packers also bought back the Atlas, Canadian Pacific and Star cannery properties in 1935 to provide wharfage and storage facilities for their fishermen.

Canning Operations

During the early 1920s can-making and canning were further automated with the introduction of the collapsed can and the vacuum closing machine. The collapsed can parts were made at a can factory and packed unformed into cartons. This greatly reduced shipping costs and storage space since seven cases of cans fit into the same size carton as one case of formed cans.

Sheets of tin were fed into the body-making machine by vacuum finger pads, and cut to the specified can size. In the stamping press the tops and bottoms were cut out, and concentric rings were stamped onto these covers to strengthen them. The covers were then passed into the curling machine where the edges were rolled, and the inside rims coated with a rubberized solution.

A reform machine in the canneries shaped the can bodies into cylinders and lock-seamed the sides. A flanging machine flanged the ends of the cylinders. Another machine double-seamed the bottoms onto the can bodies.

The Hong Wo general store with Chinese bunkhouses in the foreground and on the right. Lim Lam contracted Chinese workers for the Phoenix Cannery. They lived in the bunkhouse in front of the general store until the early 1950s. (ca. 1930)(Lam family collection)

The suzuko processing crew of the River Fish Co-operative at the foot of Number Two Road, with the Co-operative's general store in the background. (1938)(M. Kuramoto collection)

More coho, pink and chum salmon were canned during and after the First World War, as the sockeye catch declined. The expanding populations of Vancouver, Victoria, New Westminster and Nanaimo created a demand for fresh spring salmon. In the 1920s gillnetting for spring salmon began about March, followed by sockeye, pink and coho salmon, and ending with chum salmon in late fall, so the fishing and canning seasons were both greatly extended.

Henry Doyle calculated the total cost of producing a case of 96 half-pound cans of sockeye salmon at $10.96 for the 1924 season, 2.4 times the cost for the 1890s. This included $4.76 for fish, $2.18 for cans and boxes, $0.39 for labels, freight and reclamations, $0.67 for Chinese labour, $0.23 for Caucasian labour and $2.73 miscellaneous. The greatest increases were in the cost of fish (4.8 times) and the cost of miscellaneous (6.9 times). The cost of Chinese labour was unchanged because machines had replaced many workers.

The opening price for a case of 96 half-pound cans of sockeye salmon was $12.50 in 1924 and $16.00 in 1925. Thus profits between $1.54 and $5.04 per case could have been realized for the 1924 pack.

Cannery Workers

Fewer cannery workers were needed in Steveston, as canneries closed and automation increased. Japanese women replaced Native women as slimers and fillers on the canning lines, because cannery bosses found it easier to recruit Japanese women from the cannery houses along the waterfront, than to canvass Native reservations for summer help. By the 1920s most of the longhouses, sheds and huts built by the canneries to accommodate Natives were destroyed. One multiple-unit longhouse on the Phoenix Cannery premises was converted into a net shed.

While only three Chinese men were needed to operate the new butchering machine, each cannery line still required twenty to thirty Chinese workers as truckers, choppers, wipers, and bath-room crew. They were still hired by Chinese contractors and segregated in Chinese bunkhouses.

On July 1, 1923, the federal government brought in the Chinese Exclusion Act which restricted entry of Chinese immigrants into Canada to four categories: diplomats, children born in Canada, students, and merchants. Only 44 Chinese entered Canada in the following 24 years.

Salted Salmon Operations

Before 1900 canneries generally shut down for the year in mid-September. Japanese eager to exploit the fall runs of salmon had started dry-salting chum salmon in 1895 for export to Japan. Manzo Nagano settled in Victoria in the early 1890s, and operated a small hotel and a Japanese curio shop. He also started a saltery at an unknown location to process salmon. Tasaka and Shiozaki were

The interior of a salmon saltery showing concrete tanks for processing salted salmon roe (suzuko). Suzuko was packed into wooden boxes for shipment to Japan. (1938)(M. Kuramoto collection)

early processors of salted salmon, operating in the Pacific Coast Cannery. This small industry allowed many fishermen to continue fishing for salmon until the end of November. They sold their catches to salteries belonging either to fishermen's co-operatives or to private businesses. By the late 1930s there were four salmon salteries in Steveston.

River Fish Company Limited, established about 1926 at the foot of Number Two Road, was the largest co-operative with about 150 members. It distributed fresh salmon and ling cod to local markets, processed salted chum salmon and *suzuko* (salted salmon roe), and operated a general store. The chum salmon were gutted, liberally covered with dry salt, stacked on the floor for curing, and then packed in wooden boxes holding four hundred pounds. *Suzuko* was salted in concrete tanks, and then packed in boxes holding one hundred pounds. The co-operative members shared the profits from the store.

The three other Steveston salteries were Saimoto at the Imperial Cannery, S. Yoshida at the Phoenix Cannery, and G. Takahashi in a building east of the Burrard Cannery. The annual production of salted salmon between 1925 and 1938 ranged from 15,300 to 85,200 boxes. Salmon salting was prohibited by the federal government in 1939 to ensure all available salmon were canned for the war effort.

Boat Works

A 1934 census by the Japanese Fishermen's Benevolent Association (Gyosha Dantai) listed eight members in the boat building business, but some independent boat builders were not members. Sixteen boat works sites were identified on the 1936 map of the Steveston waterfront drafted by the Richmond Municipality Water Works Department.

The typical smaller boat works was usually manned by the proprietor and built only one boat each year. The Richmond Boat Works, run by Saigi Kishi, built two boats per month in boom times. It employed five carpenters full-time, and up to three more during busy periods. Most of these carpenters had apprenticed in Japan.

The standard gillnetter had become too large and heavy by the early 1920s to store inside canneries and net sheds during the winter. Several boat works had long wooden marine ways with iron rails extending into the water. On both sides of the ways were boat grids, each consisting of a series of heavy timbers on pilings set parallel to each other and perpendicular to the ways. After the fishing season ended, a boat was loaded onto a carriage on the iron rails, hauled up and shifted sideways onto a grid. By sidetracking, many gillnetters could be stored and repaired on raised timber grids near the boat works.

Map of the Steveston waterfront showing locations of boat works in 1936. (CR)

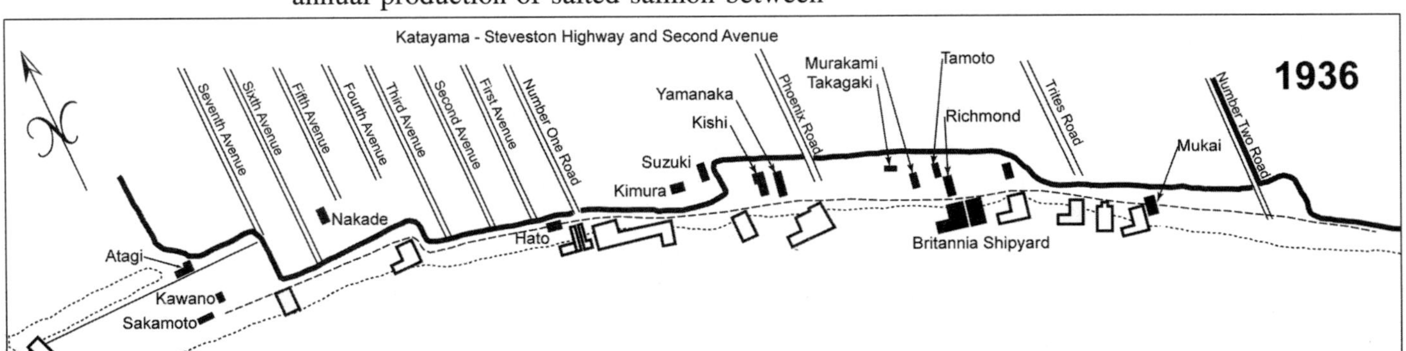

Fishing Boats

The mechanization of fishing vessels started a trend to larger vessels. The cabin was also made larger, and fitted with portholes and a second level with windows on the front and sides, and a door on the back. By the 1930s the typical Fraser River gillnetter was about 30 feet long and 7 feet 6 inches wide, with a rounded two-tiered cabin.

Larger vessels needed higher-powered engines. Easthope Brothers initially manufactured 5 HP, then 8-12 HP, 15-18 HP and eventually 30 HP engines. High-speed engines, including Lycoming, Graymarine, Palmer and Chrysler, were introduced to the Fraser River salmon gillnet fishery in the late 1930s and early 1940s.

The gillnet drum, invented by Laurie Jarvis of Sointula about 1931, revolutionized the salmon gillnet fishery by eliminating the back-breaking work of pulling in the net by hand. According to Buck Suzuki, the boat with the first gillnet drum for fishing the Fraser River was purchased by a Finnish fisherman from Sunbury about 1935. A Japanese fisherman named Onotera in the same area copied the drum and installed it in his boat a year later. Buck Suzuki was about the sixth person to have a gillnet drum on the Fraser River. Gillnet drums were common in fishing boats above the Rice Mill east of Number Five Road by 1937.

The early gillnet drum was a primitive device made of wood with a shaft through the centre and a crown pinion gear fixed at one end. The drive mechanism consisted of a long shaft fitted with a bevel gear at the drum end and a pulley at the engine-room end. A belt connected this pulley to a power-take-off on the engine. The control mechanism was a cable from the pulley end to a foot pedal in the drum well at the stern. When a fisherman pushed the foot pedal down, this pulled the belt taut and turned the drive mechanism, engaging the gillnet drum. As more of the net wrapped onto the drum, the speed of hauling

Unosuke Sakamoto's gillnetter, the first in Steveston to be powered by a high-speed Lycoming gasoline engine, with the Scottish Canadian Cannery in the background. (1937)(M. Kuramoto collection)

A fisherman loading a gillnet for the Monday morning opening. The net was repaired and treated in a bluestone tank. The net roller was temporarily stored on the fish hatch. (ca. 1938)(CVA)

Kunji Kuramoto's KAMIKAZE built by the K. Kishi Boat Works for $600 in 1939. This was one of the early gillnet boats powered by a high-speed gasoline engine. A gillnet drum was installed in this vessel the following year. (1939)(M. Kuramoto collection)

in the net increased. However, as the engine speed was set at a low number of revolutions to haul in the net, there was virtually no control of the drum speed. The crown pinion and bevel gears were soon replaced by a differential and transmission cannibalized from an abandoned automobile, allowing independent control of the drum speed.

According to Charlie Deagle, the first person in Steveston to install a gillnet drum was Kimura, who operated a boat works on the Imperial Cannery premises. He built a gillnet drum drive assembly with a car differential about 1935, but the net rollers were not fixed to the stern. During the initial trip to test the drum, Kimura quickly learned his mistake. The latter part of the net was rolling onto the drum at a rapid pace when the net rollers caught in the net and came flying into the boat, narrowly missing him.

The Lubzinski Brothers were the first people to fix two vertical rollers permanently on the stern. Fishermen guided the nets through the fixed net rollers while making a set and hauling in their net on the drum.

After many trials and corrections, which included hanging nets with slightly longer leadlines, the defects in the drum hauling system were eliminated. Fishermen in Steveston were slower to adopt the gillnet drum than upriver fishermen, because the heavy drum increased the danger of being swamped in the rough sea conditions at the river's mouth. However, most fishermen had installed gillnet drums on their boats by 1940.

Fisherman unrolling a gillnet with salmon from a gillnet drum. The drum drive assembly consisted of a differential and transmission cannibalized from an automobile. (1943) (CVA)

Wharves

By the 1920s most net wharves were completely planked, and racking and repairing of gillnets became much safer and easier.

During the fishing season gillnet boats were tied between the wharf and mooring piles. As their size and weight increased, these boats needed deeper water to stay afloat at low tides. The Steveston waterfront was probably first dredged before 1940 to deepen the harbour.

Fishing Activities

Mechanization and the larger size of the Fraser River gillnet boats greatly increased their use in other fisheries. Motorized fishing craft were first permitted in the Central Area of British Columbia's coastal waters in 1923. Natives and Caucasians had salmon fishing licenses that were valid for the entire coast, whereas Japanese with licenses for District 1 were restricted to fishing the Fraser River. In the late 1920s Native and Caucasian fishermen from the Fraser River started migrating north to fish sockeye salmon in Rivers Inlet and Smith Inlet.

Dembe Kuramoto (right) with Kamida on his combination gillnetter/ troller in Deep Bay rigged for trolling. (1939)(M. Kuramoto collection)

Japanese fishermen from Steveston started taking their gillnetters into the Straits of Georgia to handline for lingcod, troll for blueback (juvenile coho salmon) and longline for dogfish. In the 1930s five Japanese fishermen had three fishing licenses (Fraser River gillnet, handline and troll) and another twenty-two had dual licenses (Fraser River gillnet and troll.)

The handline fishery for lingcod was an important source of fresh white-fleshed fish before 1940. If a fisherman had a license to handline, his gillnet boat had a hold with holes stopped with wooden plugs. When handlining for lingcod, he pulled out the plugs and converted the hold into a live well to keep the bait and catch alive. He used a portable cabin in the stern net storage section for living quarters. He jigged or hoop-netted herring for bait, cruised to his favourite reefs and handlined for lingcod, using a mainline with a lead weight and two hooks baited with live herring. He transferred his catch to live-cages at a fishing camp. When the packer boat visited the camp to collect the fish, the fisherman killed, headed and gutted his catch. Many Japanese fishermen held only licenses for handlining, since it was permitted throughout the year, except for a short closure from January 1st to March 1st.

The blueback salmon fishery opened in mid April. To rig his boat for trolling, a fisherman added two long poles beside the mast. The poles were hinged to the deck and rested in notches on the short cross-tree near the top of the mast. The poles could be lowered outboard to 30-degree angles for fishing. To each pole the fisherman attached three cotton lines with lead weights spaced at regular intervals and five pound cannonballs on the ends. He fished with three spoons on each line, and hauled the lines by hand. A few fishermen had installed 4-spool trolling gurdies with stainless steel lines by 1940. In late June the sockeye salmon season opened, and fishermen with dual licenses changed the trolling poles for gillnets and continued gillnet fishing through late fall.

Japanese fishermen had no difficulty in obtaining licenses to fish dogfish, as few fishermen took part in this fishery. In the 1920s after the chum salmon season, these fishermen rigged their boats for longlining dogfish from January to April. Fraser River gillnet fishermen longlined for dogfish in the Straits of Georgia from off Canoe Pass in the south to Lund in the north in depths ranging from 30 to 60 fathoms. Longlining was done by hand until capstans were introduced in the late 1930s. The dogfish was rendered into fish

Miyakichi Yesaki with lingcod, red snappers and dogfish caught while longlining for dogfish near Lund. (1938)(MY)

meal and oil. The oil was used by the logging industry to grease the skids for sliding logs into bay and inlets.

In the spring of 1938, Yasuhiro 'Bill' Ezaki acted as a deck hand for Miyakichi Yesaki on a dogfishing trip to Lund. Their gillnet boat had a stern chute so they could set the longlines at full speed. They fished sixteen skates of gear. Each skate was 200 fathoms of 1/4 inch cotton or 5/8 inch manila mainline with 100 hooks spaced two fathoms apart. Using fresh or salted herring as bait, they set the longlines around four o'clock in the morning, and hauled them by hand after breakfast. They set the longlines a second time and left them soaking, while they prepared and ate lunch. Then they hauled the lines to end the day's fishing activities. They off-loaded the dogfish to a Japanese buyer stationed in the area for $6 per ton. Their provisions for the trip included a 100-pound sack of rice and various Japanese and western condiments and drinks. They fished until the 100 pounds of rice was eaten, approximately six weeks. Bill Ezaki's one-third share for this trip was $60, a sizeable wage for him at that time.

Fishermen

Racial discrimination against the Japanese increased after the First World War. The high prices and strong demand for fishery products during the war had improved the position of the Japanese fishermen. In 1919 they held 3,267 licenses, including those for deckhands. This was almost half of the licenses issued in British Columbia for that year.

Soldiers returned from the war to a dormant economy and a declining fishery. Caucasian and Native fishermen demanded an end to Japanese domination in the fishing industry. A commission of seven men headed by William Duff held hearings, and submitted a report to the Minister of Fisheries recommending that the number of salmon licenses for Japanese fishermen be reduced by 40 percent in 1923 and by 10 percent each subsequent year until all these licenses had been recovered. Some of the Japanese troll fishermen had already purchased their licenses for the year, so the reduction rate for trolling licenses was only 25 percent.

The Japanese decided to challenge this act, and filed a suit in the Supreme Court of Canada in 1927. In May 1928 the Supreme Court decision favoured the Japanese, stating that a minister did not have the discretionary power to withhold a license from a naturalized Canadian citizen. The federal government's appeal to the Privy Council was dismissed, but the government passed a law giving the Minister of Fisheries absolute discretion to issue licenses wherever the exclusive right of fishing did not already exist by law.

For some unknown reason the Minister opted to maintain the 1,242 fishing licenses given to Japanese fishermen in British Columbia in 1929. Between 1922 and 1930

1,253 Japanese fishermen lost their licenses, and by 1941 Japanese held only 12 percent of the fishing licenses.

Between 1919 and 1934 the number of Japanese fishermen with gillnet licenses on the Fraser River decreased from 874 to 400, while the number of Caucasian fishermen quadrupled from 275 to 1,105 (Appendix Table 2). Many Caucasians were unemployed workers driven into fishing during the Depression.

Japanese immigration was also reduced drastically. In 1923 the Lemieux Agreement was modified to reduce the number of Japanese male immigrants from 400 to 150 each year. Unlimited entry of wives and children continued until 1928, when the total number of Japanese immigrants per year was set at 150. There were 4,071 male and 5,325 female Japanese immigrants to Canada between 1908 and 1929.

Most Japanese adults still could not speak English, even those who had lived more than forty years in Canada. They had little opportunity or need to learn English because their helpers and fish buyers were also Japanese. The fish buyers or their English-speaking relatives helped during transactions with company and public service officials. Social intercourse was limited to the Japanese community. This heightened the Caucasion perception that the Japanese were reluctant to integrate. Increased discrimination forced the Japanese into a virtual ghetto at Steveston.

The Japanese were becoming more independent economically. Many owned their own boats and fishing gear. However, as they still did not have the right to vote, and increasing racial discrimination made their future in Canada doubtful, they continued to maintain strong ties with Japan. Many families sent their children to schools in Japan. In February 1925, when eleven crew members drowned during the visit of the training ship ***IZUMO***, fishing boats from Steveston helped dredge for the bodies in Vancouver harbour.

Whenever Japanese dignitaries visited, there were festive celebrations. In March 1937 a squadron of three airplanes and 150 decorated fishing boats gathered at the mouth of the Fraser River to greet Prince and Princess Chichibu, who arrived on the ***HEINAN MARU*** en route to the coronation of King George VI of England.

A seiner flying the Hinomaru and Union Jack, with a boat load of Steveston residents out to welcome Prince and Princess Chichibu in March 1937. (1937)(M. Kuramoto collection)

Cannery Houses

The number of cannery houses remained high in the 1930s. The Richmond Municipality Waterworks Department map of the Steveston waterfront for 1936 showed 47 buildings on the Imperial Cannery site, 55 on the Gulf of Georgia Cannery site and 23 on the Burrard Cannery site, most of which were cannery houses. Many of these houses were built on

A Japanese boy playing with a large spring salmon on the Great West Cannery wharf. (ca. 1938)(MY)

A Japanese family on the boardwalk behind a cannery house at Colonial Cannery. (ca. 1939)(MY)

pilings outside the main dyke, so the wharf and boardwalk were the backyard and playground for the families.

Wood was readily available for cooking and heating the houses. Fishermen kept a constant lookout for logs all year, towed them in and tied them to the boardwalk bulkhead. During the sunny days of winter they sawed the logs and chopped them into firewood blocks. Occasionally, fishermen would visit the log booms of New Westminster on their gillnetters to collect bark off pine logs before the logs were cut into lumber.

On rainy days and evenings fishermen and their wives often made gillnets for spring and chum salmon, while the children filled the needles with linen twine. They generally bought machine-made gillnets with smaller mesh for sockeye salmon from the canneries.

Men splitting a large slice of a tree trunk into firewood along the dyke at the Great West Cannery. Firewood was used in cast iron stoves for cooking, in tin sheet stoves for heating, and in fireplaces under Japanese baths. (ca. 1939)(MY)

The Years of Upheaval

Chapter

6

1940 - 1949

Main Channel of the Fraser River

The Department of Marine continued to expand and repair the jetties installed on the main channel. The original pilings of the North Jetty and the western end of the Woodwards Training Wall were replaced with boulders. A boulder jetty was extended out seaward from the western end of Albion Dyke No. 1.

Townsite and Waterfront

In 1941 Steveston was the largest settlement in Richmond with a permanent population of approximately 4,000 people. There were 30 percent more businesses in the town site than in 1930. The British Columbia and Yukon Directory for 1941 listed forty-three Japanese and twenty-eight Caucasian enterprises. Hong Wo General Store and the Sun Cafe were the only remaining Chinese firms.

Then disaster struck, initiating a chain of events that altered Steveston permanently. Japan had invaded China in 1938. By 1939 Germany had occupied Czechoslavakia, Austria and Poland, precipitating the Second World War. Canada had supported Britain and her allies against Germany since September 10, 1939. On December 7, 1941, the Japanese Imperial Navy attacked Pearl Harbour in Hawaii, and destroyed 18 ships at the American Naval base there. This attack shocked everyone, and devastated the Japanese living in Canada.

On December 8, 1941, Canada declared war on Japan. Responding to fears that the coastal Japanese communities would help Japan invade British Columbia, the federal government immediately arrested 31 Japanese-Canadian community leaders, and ordered the closure of three Japanese papers published in Vancouver and all Japanese language schools in the province. Then it confiscated all Japanese-owned fishing boats in the province and had them towed to New Westminster for safekeeping.

On January 14, 1942, the federal government declared the Japanese to be enemy aliens, and ordered the evacuation and relocation from the west coast of all Japanese males over the age of eighteen. On February

Moncton Street facing west on Number One Road. With about seventy-one businesses, Steveston was the largest town in Richmond before the Second World War. (1942)(VPL)

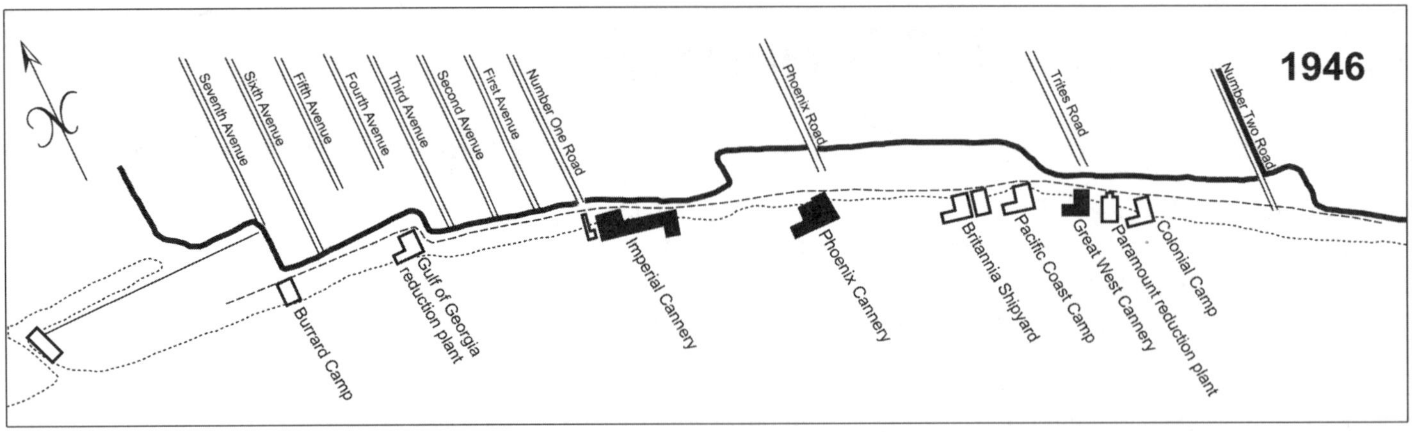

Map of the Steveston waterfront showing locations of canneries in 1946. (solid buildings - operating; clear buildings - not operating) (IAO)

26, 1942, the evacuation order was extended to include Japanese women and children. The complete evacuation from Steveston of 2,600 Japanese residents by May 1942 left Steveston almost a ghost town with only one-third of its small businesses and its population.

The number of students attending Lord Byng School dropped from 550 to 137, then climbed again as children of Boeing aircraft workers at Sea Island were brought in by bus, and Native families arrived from Northern British Columbia to take over the fishing and canning jobs vacated by the Japanese.

The Canadian Armed Forces had established Fort Steveston in October 1939 at the west end of Steveston Highway. This fort was one of four protecting Vancouver and the Sea Island Airport from possible attack by German and Japanese forces. The threat was not imaginary. In May 1942 a German submarine was sighted by George Fentiman from the Sand Heads Lightship. Eighty men in the 58th Battery manned the fort and its two 18-pounder field guns until January 1944. Japan officially surrendered to the Allied Forces on September 2, 1945, four months after Germany's surrender on May 7, 1945.

On November 23, 1946, the fourteen-room Lord Byng School burned down. Students had to go on double shift until it was reconstructed exactly the same. Older students went to the former Japanese kindergarten on Chatham Street.

By 1948 newcomers had rebuilt Steveston to a town of thirty-seven businesses, all owned by Caucasians. The government of Canada did not allow any person of Japanese descent within 100 miles of the west coast until April 1949. Most of the approximately 250 Japanese-Canadian families that eventually settled in Steveston had returned by 1951.

Development of the Commercial Fishing Industry

The International Pacific Salmon Commission established in 1937 completed its required eight years of investigations. In late 1944 it initiated a series of projects to build fish ladders at Hell's Gate and other sites on the Fraser River system. By the following spring the right bank fishway and the lower section of the left bank fishway at Hell's Gate were almost completed. These fishways improved the passage of fish during the 1945 season. Escapements of Stuart, Horsefly, late Stuart and Stellako River salmon were five times greater than in the 1941 brood year. There were 5.0 fishing days per week until 1945, when the Commission started imposing fishing closures to help endangered runs increase to previous levels.

In spite of the disruptions caused by the Japanese evacuation, the remaining Fraser River fishermen caught 8.8 million salmon in 1942, more than twice the yield of the previous dominant year of 1938. The average annual catch for the off-years was 2.0 million during this decade. There were slightly over 1,000 fishing boats from 1945 to 1948, except in 1946 when about 8.3 million sockeye were caught by 1,800 fishermen, including hundreds of gillnet fishermen arriving from the central and northern coasts to share in the exceptional Adams River run. Canadian fishermen captured 63 percent of the total Fraser River sockeye catch in the 1940s.

Steveston Canneries and Other Waterfront Enterprises

The Imperial, Phoenix and Great West

Canneries canned salmon during this period. Under Wartime Controls 70 percent of British Columbia's salmon pack of 1941 was sent to Great Britain. The Imperial and Gulf of Georgia Canneries also canned herring from 1939 to 1945. Canned salmon and herring were among the staple foods of soldiers during the Second World War. The Imperial Cannery actually canned 1,811,947 48-pound cases of herring from 1939 to 1945, compared with 1,172,252 cases of salmon. The total production of canned herring in British Columbia from 1939 to 1945 was 6,228,995 cases, and almost 30 percent of this was produced by the Imperial Cannery. A tin of herring in tomato sauce sold for 11.5 cents at the Hudson's Bay Company store in 1942.

In 1946 BC Packers built a reduction plant to process herring. The Imperial, Gulf of Georgia and Phoenix Canneries and Nelson Bros. Fishing Company all operated reduction plants to render herring to fishmeal, oil and solubles. The fishmeal was used to make high protein feed for cattle, hogs and poultry. The oil was used to make cosmetics, paints and lubricants, and the solubles were used in plant-feeding liquids. After the war soldiers returning home to Steveston recalled eating Steveston herring and using herring oil to lubricate their machine guns.

Cannery Workers

Much of the work on the sliming and canning lines prior to 1942 was done by Japanese women. After the Japanese evacuation from the coast, Native women from reservations along the coast and Caucasian women from the lower mainland were recruited for this work.

Boat Works

All the boat works except the Britannia Shipyard were operated by Japanese boatbuilders until 1942, when the Japanese were evicted from Steveston. There was little demand for new fishing boats immediately after the Japanese evacuation in 1942, because all the Japanese boats were available for purchase.

Few new vessels were constructed during

An aerial view of the Phoenix Cannery, with boat ways of the abandoned Yamanaka Boat Works and cannery houses on the extreme left. (1946)(CRA)

Salmon gillnet and codfish boats seized from Japanese fishermen and impounded at Annieville dyke near New Westminister. The gillnetters have gillnet drums or net wells and the codfish boats have cabins forward and aft. (1942)(UBC-SP)

Map of the Steveston waterfront showing locations of boat works in 1946.

the war because the massive transfer of resources to the war effort left little for the development of national industries. However, by 1946 there were eight boat works in Steveston, all operated by Caucasians. Among them were Mike David, who took over the Atagi Boat Works at Garry Point, and the Lubzinski brothers who operated the Kishi Boat Works at the Phoenix Cannery. There were also Marshall and Markstrom who occupied the Mukai Boat Works at the foot of Second Avenue, and Stoltz Brothers at the Nakade Boat Works on Seventh Avenue. Allan Steves, grandson of Manoah, worked for several years at David Boat Works, and then opened Steves Boat Works at the west end of Steveston Highway.

One newcomer, Geiri Sigurgeirson, was a skilled craftsman descended from a long line of Icelandic boatbuilders. He had completed two boats at Prince Rupert, but decided to settle in Steveston with his wife and six children in 1943. He set up a boat building shop in his back yard on Fourth Avenue and soon had several contracts from fishermen who admired his first Steveston boat ***The TEMPEST***. His brother Joe Sigurgeirson rented the Katayama boathouse at Second Avenue and Steveston Highway and began building boats there in 1946.

Fishing Boats

The Japanese fishing boats were impounded immediately after Pearl Harbour, and later taken to New Westminster. Realizing how the seizure of 1,337 boats would affect

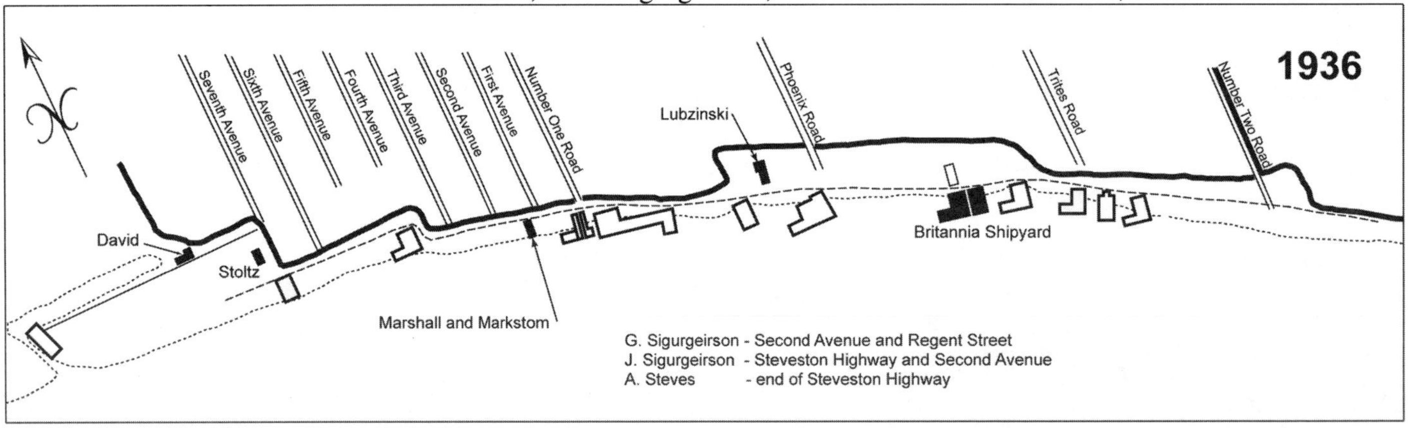

the 1942 salmon catch, the government authorized a committee to sell the confiscated boats to non-Japanese at "fair market prices". These boats included 860 gillnetters, 148 packers, 141 cod boats, 120 trollers and 68 seiners. Of these 887 were sold. J.H. Todd and Sons purchased 14 gillnetters ranging in cost from $600 to $1,500 during February and March of 1942. This company also purchased 9 seiners, including the ***HOWE SOUND III*** for $12,500. The Board of Marine Underwriters of San Francisco estimated the replacement value of this boat at $16,000. The sales agreements required the vendors to pay for any repairs that the purchasers deemed necessary to make the boats seaworthy and in good running order.

The Fraser River gillnetter developed rapidly after the Japanese evacuation. Fraser River fishermen were expanding into new salmon fishing grounds during the Second World War, and they needed larger, wider vessels with greater sea-worthiness and higher load capacities. Consider the vessels owned by Bob Karliner. He purchased the ***CHALLENGER***, his third boat, from the Fishing Vessel Disposal Committee for $750 in 1942. This boat was 31 feet 6 inches in length, 7 feet 6 inches in breadth and was powered with a 2-cylinder, 14 HP Palmer gasoline engine. In 1944 Karliner contracted the Lubzinski brothers to build his first new boat, the ***MODERN BEAUTY***, for $3,200. This gillnetter measured 33 feet in length, 8 feet 6 inches in breadth, and was powered with a 3-cylinder, 20 HP Easthope engine. Three years later, Karliner replaced this vessel with the ***ELSIE K No. 1*** built by the Stoltz brothers. This vessel was powered with a 6-cylinder, high-speed 110 HP Chrysler gasoline engine. It was 35 feet in length, 10 feet in breadth and cost $7,200. In five years the Fraser River gillnetter had increased in length by 3 feet and breadth by 2 feet 6 inches. The flared bow, square stern and enlarged cabin with sufficient headroom for a person to stand upright became standard features on Fraser River gillnetters.

Wharves

Net floats were introduced in the 1940s to provide space for net racks and moorage for larger boats in deeper tidal waters. The Phoenix pond was dredged about 1947 to accommodate larger boats. Here gillnetters could be tied directly to boat floats, making access to boats at moorage much easier and safer, as ladders were replaced with ramps.

In the late 1940s an elevator was developed to haul boats out of the water for winter storage and repairs. This system was quicker, easier and required less space than iron rails on wooden ways.

Bob Karliner's ***ELSIE K*** *No. 1 ready for launching from the Stoltz Brothers Boat Works. The gillnetters were hauled out for painting and repairs before the salmon fishing season. (1949) (B. Karliner collection)*

Fishing Activities

During the war there was an unlimited demand for all species of canned salmon. In the fall of 1944 Fraser River gillnetters started fishing chum salmon near Qualicum in the Straits of Georgia. Fifteen gillnetters from the river were the only ones fishing this area in

*Sherman McDonald's **VALERIE** on the boat hoist at the Gulf of Georgia Cannery. This vessel was built by P. Sather in 1946 and powered by a 2-cylinder Heaps gasoline engine. (ca. 1949)(S. McDonald collection)*

Cannery row from the Gulf of Georgia showing the Star Camp and Imperial Cannery in the background, a ramp in the foreground and gillnetters moored perpendicular to the net floats. (1948)(S. McDonald collection)

the falls of 1944, 1945 and 1946.

Fraser River fishermen continued to adapt their gillnetters for new uses. Bob Karliner and his deck hand on the ***CHALLENGER*** started fishing dogfish by setting coiled longlines. They hauled each longline by taking a half turn around the revolving drum core and coiling the line manually. They soon switched to hauling the longline onto the drum and tucking the hooks under the line. They baited the hooks with pieces of herring, as they reeled the longline off the drum to set it. The gillnet drum eliminated the back-breaking task of pulling the longline hand over hand, so they were able to fish 5,000 hooks a day.

During the Second World War the price of dogfish liver increased from 10 cents to $1.50 per pound. The liver provided vitamins A and D before the mass production of synthetic vitamins in the late 1940s. In April 1945 Karliner and his deck hand fished off Namu with the ***MODERN BEAUTY***. Dogfish were especially thick, feeding on herring concentrated on the spawning grounds in Burke Channel. With cash buyers paying 20 cents per pound for dogfish livers, the two men grossed $1,000 in two weeks of longlining.

After fishing dogfish, they cruised north to Hecate Straits for the May 1st opening for halibut. They operated out of Squarderee Cove on Stephen's Island along with four other gillnetters. They fished the Two-Peaks grounds of Hecate Straits, halfway between Triple Island and the Rose Spit buoy, with seven to eight skates of longlines with 1,300 hooks. They set the longline two or three times each fishing day, using fresh or frozen herring as bait. In one month they made $1,500. Bob Karliner on the ***MODERN BEAUTY*** and Nick Mardich on the ***BARBARA M*** were the first Fraser River gillnetters to fish halibut in Hecate Straits. Increasing numbers of Fraser River gillnetters participated in this fishery in the 1950s.

Fraser River gillnetters off Qualicum Beach fishing for chum salmon in the fall. (ca. 1945)(B. Karliner collection)

*Bob Karliner longlining for halibut in Hecate Strait on his **MODERN BEAUTY.** (1945)(B. Karliner collection)*

Fishermen

Many Japanese fishermen had built their own homes by 1941, and were vacating the cannery houses. They also got more involved in the berry and vegetable growing industries of Richmond. In 1941 there were 55 Japanese families registered with the Richmond Berry Growers Association with a total area under cultivation of 122 acres of berries and 225 acres of vegetables. Not all the farming Japanese were members of this association.

After the Japanese families were evacuated, the fishing companies actively recruited fishermen from the west coast reservations, and the east coast and lake fisheries, but the number of people that moved to Steveston never equaled the number of the displaced Japanese.

Japanese Evacuation

In 1942 between February and October 21,460 Japanese people were displaced from their homes on the west coast. About 17,000 of these were Canadian citizens. The Japanese in Steveston were given two months to prepare to leave. Each person was allowed to take two suitcases of personal clothing and effects, about fifty pounds. The Japanese had to surrender the remainder of their belongings, including their homes and furniture, in trust with the Custodian of Alien Property. A few asked non-Japanese neighbours to look after their houses, and store some valued possessions.

The Japanese were transported by train from Steveston directly to their final relocation sites. Unlike families from settlements along the coast, they were spared the indignity of temporary internment at the livestock barns at Exhibition Gardens in Vancouver's Hastings Park. Families wishing to stay together "volunteered" as labourers for the sugar beet farms of Alberta and Manitoba. Other families anxious to remain as near to the coast as possible "chose" to be evacuated to a new settlement at Tashme, and ghost towns like Minto, Kaslo, New Denver and Lemon Creek in the interior of British Columbia. Many able-bodied men from this latter group were taken by train with two or three days notice. The women and children went later.

The Japanese were forced to pay for their own incarceration. On January 19, 1943, the federal government authorized the Custodian of Alien Property to liquidate all Japanese properties held under protective custody. Thus the Japanese lost all the worldly assets they had accumulated over fifty years of hard toil in Canada, including their homes, businesses, farms, boats and fishing gear.

The Japanese had no prominent leader to defend them against the public racism and government discrimination generated by the air attack on Pearl Harbour. They quietly complied en masse as the government imposed a strict curfew, arrested their most visible citizens, shut down their newspapers and language schools, confiscated and sold their boats, evicted them from their homes, and received their properties in trust, then sold them to defray the cost of their evacuation. The Japanese obeyed the laws of the country, even though these laws stripped away their most basic civil rights. There was not one documented act of sabotage during the war by either the Japanese who had immigrated to Canada (Issei) or their children born in Canada (Nisei, Sansei).

The Japanese were relocated to the interior of Canada, to regions completely foreign to them. They were thrown into primitive accommodations. In many of the interior towns the men were still building makeshift three-room houses for eight people when the women and children arrived. For months their only light was from candles, their drinking water hauled by hand from streams a mile away.

The children were taught by correspondence courses and older students, instead of qualified teachers, unless they were lucky enough to be near a sympathetic religious school. Hideko Hyodo, the only Japanese teacher who had taught at Lord Byng School, helped organize and supervise school instruction for Japanese children in seven British Columbia internment camps.

The Franciscan Sisters of the Atonement arranged for the relocation of some Japanese families to Greenwood in the Kootenays. A few of the Sisters accompanied the evacuees to Greenwood and continued to teach and help them.

Homes built by Japanese fishermen along Dyke Road east of Number Two Road in 1940, with private wharves and net houses for mooring gillnet boats and repairing, treating and storing fishing gear. (ca. 1940) (MY)

Miyakichi Yesaki purchased the ***EBB TIDE*** *for $3,000 after returning to the coast. This boat was powered by a 4-cylinder, 96 HP Graymarine engine. (1950)(MY)*

At the end of the war government officials tried to persuade the Japanese to return to Japan by subsidizing their return fare, but most of them wanted to remain Canadians. Only 4,000 accepted this offer. The remaining Japanese in the British Columbia interior were given the option of relocating to the other provinces at government expense.

Return of the Japanese

On June 15, 1948, the government of Canada gave the Japanese the right to vote, and on March 31, 1949, the British Columbia legislature passed an elections act giving the vote to the Japanese, and allowing them to return to the coast. In May 1949 the federal Department of Marine and Fisheries repealed the act prohibiting persons of Japanese ancestry from holding fishing licenses. The fishing companies soon started recruiting Japanese fishermen. Ken Fraser of British Columbia Packers and Shinichi Matsuo made several trips to the interior of British Columbia and to Alberta to entice former fishermen to return.

Many smaller fishermen's unions had joined together in 1945 to form the United Fishermen and Allied Workers Union. Soon after the announcement of May 1949, Homer Stevens, Bill Rigby and other officials of the UFAWU met with Buck Suzuki, George Tanaka, Seiji Homma and Unosuke Sakamoto of the Japanese Canadian Citizens Association (JCCA). They agreed that any Japanese wishing to resume fishing should do so through the UFAWU. Union officials pledged support for the return of Japanese fishermen if these fishermen did not return en masse, and if they did not organize a separate bargaining bloc. A resolution supporting this policy was approved by the UFAWU convention later that month. Twenty-eight Japanese fishermen returned to fish the Fraser River in 1949. At first union officials had to intervene in several minor racial conflicts on the Steveston waterfront. The support of Homer Stevens and the UFAWU for returning Japanese was instrumental in their rapid and relatively innocuous integration back into the fisheries.

Most of the returning Japanese had fished before the evacuation. During the war many had been herded into interior ghost towns with little opportunity for employment. Others had been interned on sugar beet farms on the prairies more or less as indentured labourers. They barely earned enough to live during the eight years of the evacuation. The Japanese had essentially been robbed of eight of their most productive years. They had lost everything they had accumulated in Canada, except the fifty pounds each person was allowed to take for relocation. These returning fishermen, most in their thirties, forties and fifties, had to begin a new life with little more than what they had carried away eight years previously.

In 1942 the Japanese fishermen generally had the most modern and well maintained boats. Most of the returning Japanese fishermen purchased used boats, many of which had been confiscated from the Japanese at the outbreak of the war. They had to start

A Gulf of Georgia Cannery house inhabited by a Caucasian family during the Second World War. (1950)(S. McDonald collection)

all over again with generally obsolete pre-war boats. These boats were serviceable for the Fraser River, but inadequate for up-coast fishing grounds and other fisheries. The primary aim of these fishermen was to buy standard gillnetters, capable of fishing the entire coast and operating several types of fishing gears. Most had replaced their vessels within three years of returning to the coast.

Cannery Houses

Many Native fishermen and their families stayed in the cannery houses during the salmon fishing season. Some Caucasian fishermen and their families also moved into cannery houses. By 1949 most of these fishermen had moved out of the cannery houses and into their own homes. Many of the cannery houses remained empty and others were destroyed during the 1940s, including those at Canadian Pacific camp.

The fishing companies did not rent cannery houses to Japanese fishermen in 1949. The first returning fishermen left their families behind and lived in hotels for several weeks while they looked for boats and gear. Unosuke Sakamoto was able to rent a cannery house-boat, which was not classified as a house because it floated on water. His family joined him soon after. Fishermen without families lived on their boats during the salmon fishing season. Mrs. Sakamoto frequently cooked for ten to fifteen of these fishermen at a time. Other fishermen stayed with Japanese who had purchased their own homes.

The Years of Renewal

Chapter 7

1950 - 1974

Sand Heads lighthouse constructed off the western extremity of the North Jetty. (ca. 1980)(J. Yamanaka photo)

Main Channel of the Fraser River

The Department of Public Works completed replacing the wooden North Jetty with a wall of boulders and extended the boulder wall from the Albion No. 1 Dyke to the Number 16 buoy in the 1950s.

Two rock jetties were constructed in 1955 to provide better protection for the Steveston waterfront. One jetty extended from the Canadian Pacific site to the upstream end of Shady (Steveston) Island, and the other was on the Steveston sand bar facing the waterfront. The upstream jetty effectively cut off the water flow, creating a body of stagnant water in the channel. Later, rocks from the top of the jetty were removed to lower the jetty level so water could flush the channel at high tide. The rock breakwater, built on the Steveston sand bar which had formed naturally over the past fifty years, prevented boats from crossing the bar, protected the harbour, and more clearly defined the Steveston Channel.

SAND HEADS No. 16 was driven ashore by severe storms on many occasions during its 42-year service off the mouth of the Fraser River. The lightship was finally withdrawn from service after being driven ashore onto Point Roberts in November 1957. The Department of Transport replaced the lightship with a fixed station at the western extremity of North Jetty in 1960. The two-storey, 34-foot by 46-foot lighthouse was supported on eight concrete pilings. Two, 2-man crews manned the lighthouse on a rotational basis.

Town Site and Waterfront

The population of the lower mainland increased substantially after the Second World War, as soldiers returned and immigrants arrived from war-ravaged Europe. Richmond changed from an agricultural community to a suburban community. Most of the large farms in the west half of Lulu Island were subdivided and filled with single-family homes. Richmond became a bedroom community for Vancouver. The first multi-family units were built in Steveston. About 200 townhouse units called Mariner's Village were built around 1970 between Seventh Avenue and the dyke along Sturgeon Banks.

The Steveston to Sydney service via the Gulf Islands on the ferry ***MOTOR PRINCESS*** was discontinued in 1950. From February 1954 to September 1958 the Coast Ferries Service, initiated by Sparkie New, operated between Steveston and the southern Gulf Islands. The ***LADY ROSE*** carried passengers

The Coast Ferries office and waiting room for the ferry ***LADY ROSE*** *on Bowditch wharf at the foot of Number Two Road. Bowditch was the postmaster at London's Landing from 1901 to 1924. (1971)(MY)*

Map of the Steveston waterfront showing the estimated extent of Shady Island in 1895, 1911, 1946 and 1971.

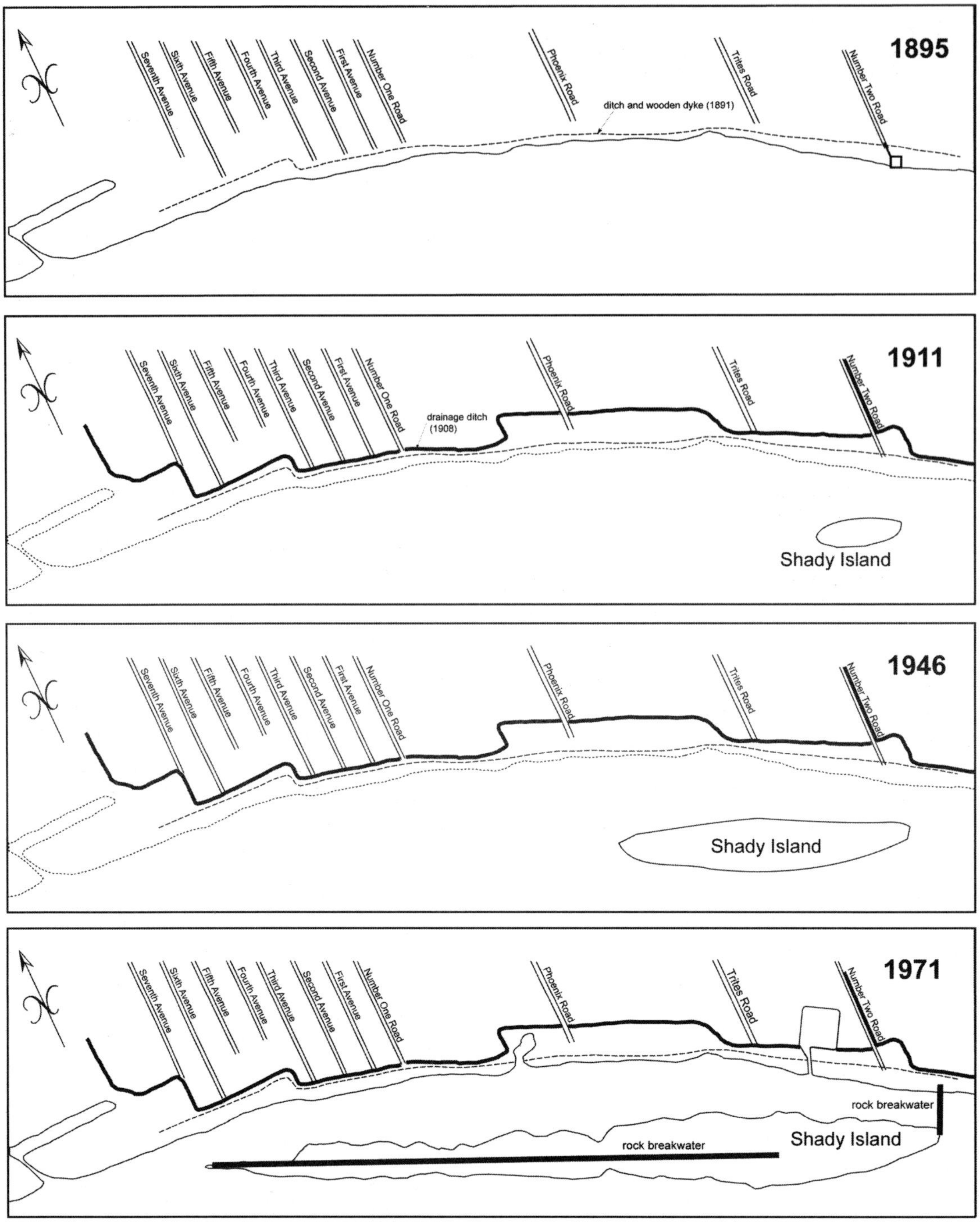

and one automobile from Bowditch Wharf at the foot of Number Two Road to Galiano, Mayne and Saturna Islands.

The road system in Richmond was expanded and improved. The steel and concrete Oak Street Bridge connected Lulu Island with the mainland in 1957, and in the following year the British Columbia Electric Railway Company tram to Steveston was replaced with buses. In May 1959 the Deas Island Tunnel, later renamed the George Massey Tunnel, provided Richmond with a direct link to Delta. The ferry ***DELTA PRINCESS*** made the last crossing between Ladner and Woodward's Landing on the day the tunnel was opened.

There were few changes in businesses along the main streets of Steveston. Only seven Japanese businesses were established in the 1950s, including three small groceries, two garages, a radio shop and a jewellery store. In the late 1960s a new shopping mall at Richmond Centre (formerly Brighouse) with two large department stores, Sears and Hudson's Bay Company, and smaller shopping malls at Broadmoor and Seafair attracted many

Steveston residents, but most still bought their groceries and hardware in their home town.

The Steveston Community Society, formed in 1946, bought land across Moncton Street from the Imperial Cannery, and raised money to build the Steveston Community Centre in 1957 and the Japanese Martial Arts Building in 1971. Their property included Tom Leslie's store and tram ticket office at Number One and Moncton, a Steveston landmark from 1929 to 1975.

Development of the Commercial Fishery

From 1950 to 1968 the numbers of fishing vessels on the Fraser River averaged about 1,400. After the Davis plan to limit the number of fishing licenses and a buy-back program were implemented in 1968, the number of vessels dropped to about 1,100. However, the efficiency of the fishing fleet increased, and the International Pacific Salmon Commission had to reduce the number of fishing days from an average of 5.1 days per week during the 1950s to 2.6 days per week during the first half of the 1970s.

Between 1950 and 1974 the Fraser River produced an average of 6.2 million sockeye salmon per year in dominant cycle years, and 3.6 million in the off-cycle years. The highest catch was 14.9 million fish in 1958.

Canneries and Other Waterfront Enterprises

Prospects for the salmon fishing industry in the 1950s were higher than at any time since the early 1890s. Canada and the United States had agreed to divide the Fraser River catch equally. Canning companies expected greater salmon returns, strong demand and high prices for canned salmon. With a promising future, they invested heavily to up-grade their facilities.

Paramount Cannery (1957)

The Nelson Brothers Fisheries bought out Great West, which closed in 1956, and built the Paramount Cannery to replace its St. Mungo Cannery further up the Fraser River. Nelson Brothers had also owned and operated northern British Columbia canneries since 1934. The Paramount was the first new Steveston cannery in fifty years, and the only Steveston cannery built on landfill instead of pilings. It had a floor area of 24,000 square feet.

A downstream aerial view of the Steveston waterfront and Shady Island with newly constructed rock jetties. The level of the top jetty was lowered to permit flushing of Steveston Channel at high water.(1955)(CRA)

An aerial view of cannery row: from the left, the Great West Cannery, the Paramount Cannery and Herring Reduction Plant (formerly the Brick Factory) and the Colonial Cannery. The cannery houses above the Colonial Cannery were occupied by Japanese families in the 1950s. (ca. 1956)(CRA)

The Paramount Cannery was the most modern plant at the time. Its six canning lines had the ability to produce 1,250 cans per minute. Theoretically it could produce 12,500 cases of 48 cans in a single eight hour day, the amount a cannery in 1890 took an entire year to pack.

Ice was first used by the troll fishery for holding and transporting spring and coho salmon to fresh fish markets. Salmon caught by gillnetters and seiners were transported without ice by catcher or packer boats to the nearby canneries. In the early 1960s the refrigerated sea water system was developed to facilitate bulk holding and transporting of salmon. The ten refrigerated tanks of the Paramount Cannery could hold between 350,000 and 400,000 pounds of fish. With seawater chilled to 30 degrees Fahrenheit and antibiotics added to the water, fish could be kept in these tanks for up to fourteen days. Packer boats with refrigerated seawater could transport large volumes of fish over long distances. With less need to have canneries near the fishing grounds, marginal canneries were closed and many cannery operations were centralized and consolidated.

Three canneries processed salmon on the Steveston waterfront in the 1950s and 1960s. The Phoenix Cannery and the Paramount Cannery processed only salmon and herring, and were idle for much of the year. BC Packers operated the Imperial Cannery throughout the year. Besides canning salmon in summer and reducing herring, it canned oysters and clams during the winter and early spring, and canned tuna when the retorts were not used for salmon canning. The Imperial started processing bottomfish in the 1950s, filleting sole, cod and Pacific ocean perch. It also processed halibut, principally through April, May and June.

Freezing gained rapid and wide acceptance as a means of preserving food because it cost less than canning. Furthermore, freezing did not appreciably alter the natural state of the product. Good quality fish were generally selected for freezing, and the remainder used for canning. The new Imperial processing, freezing and storage plant opened September 20, 1966, adjacent to the cannery. It employed 450 people and processed 40 million pounds of fish each year. The bottomfish operation became its most important activity in the 1960s and 1970s.

In 1968, plagued with financial difficulties, the New England Fishing Company closed the Phoenix Cannery, formerly owned by ABC Company, and sold the property to BC Packers. In the same year, both the Paramount Cannery and the Nelson Brothers herring reduction plant were taken over and shut down by BC Packers. The closures of the Phoenix and Paramount Canneries resulted from consolidation of ownership, and technological changes including the evolution of high-speed fully automated canning lines and the development of refrigeration systems.

In 1969 Garfield-Weston of Britain purchased BC Packers. This multinational

The Phoenix Cannery, shut down in 1969 after 72 years of operation. (1971)(MY)

food company also owned Kelly-Douglas, Malkins, Loblaws, 5,600 supermarkets and 300 food processing mills.

BC Packers and the Canadian Fishing Company operated their herring reduction plants after 1971 to process roe herring carcasses. Non-operating canneries, including the Gulf of Georgia, the Pacific Coast and the Colonial Canneries, were converted into net storage sheds. These buildings, erected in the 1890s, still remained on the Steveston waterfront in 1990s because they were re-roofed and re-sided, and their interiors were remodelled during the 1950s. The Phoenix building was essentially not used after its canning lines and reduction plant closed.

Canning Operations

The August 1957 issue of Western Fisheries described the building, equipment and operations of the new Paramount Cannery. Canning here was a high-speed, continuous, highly automated process. The machinery was completely powered by electricity and hydraulics. One of the butchering machines was capable of processing 140 fish per minute, twice the rate of the other two machines. There were 850 feet of aluminum conveyors to move fish from the holding tanks to the filling stations, and 200 feet of elevators and conveyors to move empty and filled cans. The conveyors and elevators were driven by 130 electric motors. The five retorts in this plant were the largest of any salmon cannery on the British Columbia coast.

The six canning lines were arranged to process fish in a straight line from unloading whole fish to stacking canned fish into boxes. They could produce one-pound, half-pound and quarter-pound cans.

Fish were brailed from packers into four sorters on the Paramount wharf. Fish were sorted, weighed and routed to ten seawater holding tanks, chilled to about 30 degrees Fahrenheit by Freon refrigeration machinery. From the holding tanks, fish were conveyed to the butchering machines. The carcasses went to the washing tables where workers cleaned slime and blood clots from the body cavities. The cleaned fish were transported to the gang knives and cut into steaks. Workers inspected the steaks and cut the larger ones into smaller chunks. These chunks passed to the filling machines and were pushed into cans.

Map of the Steveston waterfront showing locations of canneries in 1971, (solid buildings - operating: clear buildings - not operating) (CR)

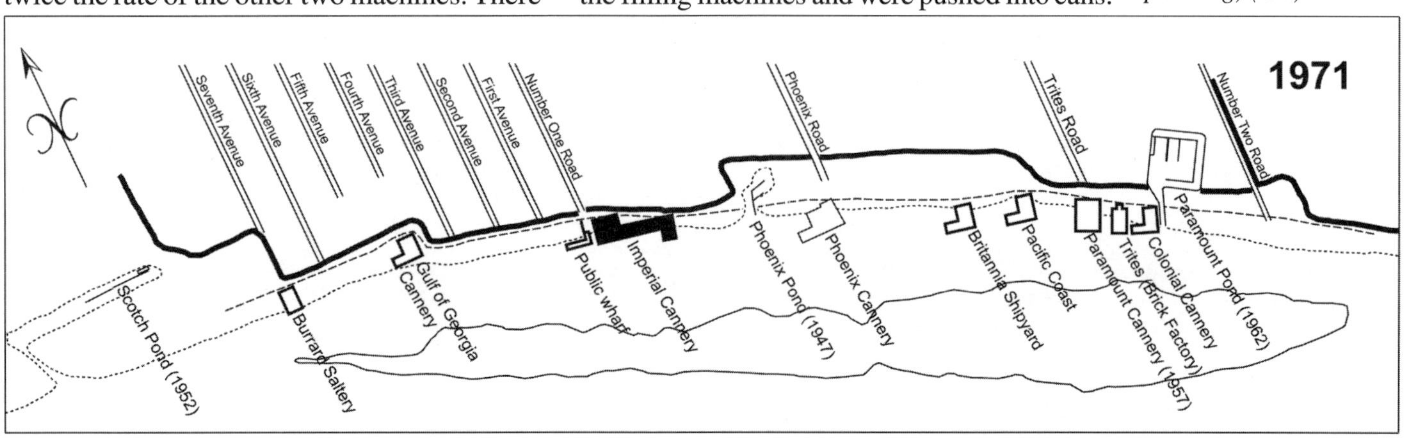

The Pacific Coast Cannery, used as a camp for part of the BC Packers gillnet fleet. (1971)(MY)

Filled cans were then passed to the salting machine and seeded with salt, and to the automatic weighing machine where underweight cans were ejected to one side and filled. The cans then travelled to the topping machine where the tops were clamped on loosely. They were next conveyed to the vacuum closing machine, where air was evacuated from the cans, and the tops sealed tight.

As the sealed cans came off the canning lines, they were scooped onto a cooler in a Busse truck by a worker with an L-shaped rod. The filled cooler was lowered by a hydraulic lift so another cooler could be placed on top to be filled. When the Busse trucks were full, twelve trucks were rolled into each retort, where the canned salmon were cooked under pressure for ninety minutes. Then the pressure was dropped, and cool water was fed into the retorts through the steam pipes for about ten minutes, and then drained. The Busse trucks were rolled out and the cans unloaded for labelling and boxing.

Cannery Workers

Caucasian men and women continued to dominate the cannery work force. When the Japanese returned to the coast, Japanese women again became prominent on the canning lines. Very few Native women and Chinese men were still employed in the canneries by the late 1960s. The pre-war Chinese immigrants were retiring from the labour force. The Chinese bunkhouses at the Imperial Cannery and the Hong Wo store were last occupied in the 1950s.

Boat Works

After 1949 many of the Japanese boat building families returned and established new boat works, including Nakade, Atagi, Kishi, Yamanaka, Sakamoto and Mukai. There was an increasing demand for new boats by the Japanese returning to the coast and by Natives

*The Gulf of Georgia Cannery, which processed herring into meal and oil until 1979. In the foreground, Kaz Hirata's **JEWEL** built by G. Sigurgeirson and George Sturgeon. (1950) (H. Hirata collection)*

and Caucasians eager to up-grade to larger vessels. The Nakade Boat Works was the most prolific boat works in Steveston during the 1950s and 1960s, launching up to ten boats a year.

Wood was the only material used for construction of small boats at the start of the 1950s. Red and yellow cedars from the west coast were used for planking and bulkheads, respectively. Oak from the east coast was used for the ribs. However, by the 1970s fine-grained, old-growth cedar planking was becoming rare and costly. Scarcity of skilled shipwrights, and increasing labour costs forced builders of wooden boats to look for alternative building materials. They had to reduce either material costs or maintenance costs of new boats. Some builders started producing fibreglass-reinforced plastic (FRP) boats in the 1950s and aluminum boats in the 1960s. By 1971 there were about seven wooden boatworks and 3 FRP boat works (Garren, Stoltz, Yamanaka). One aluminum boat works, ALU-CRAFT, was established by Kurt Csontala in Steveston in 1971.

Fishing Boats

In the 1950s Steveston boat works were operating at maximum capacity building standard gillnetters, which were wooden boats measuring 35 feet in length, 10 feet in breadth and powered with high speed, gasoline engines.

Boat builders began experimenting with different hull designs and construction materials. Several boat works used marine plywood or mahogany planks to build planing hull boats. The hulls were coated with layers of fibreglass mats impregnated with plastic resins. These wood/FRP combination craft

The Nakade Boat Works with ways and grid for hauling out boats. The last boat was built by this boat works in 1972. The building was torn down in 1973. (1971)(MY)

The Kishi Boat Works, the last on the Steveston waterfront to build wooden boats. The building was closed in 1985, and set on fireby vandals and destroyed in 1989. (1971)(MY)

were heavy and never gained widespread acceptance.

The Stoltz Brothers Boat Works built the ***ZIRCON***, a vessel with a V planing hull in 1952. The hull was cedar-planked with wedge seams and was not caulked. The fuel tanks,

Map of the Steveston waterfront showing locations of boat works in 1971.

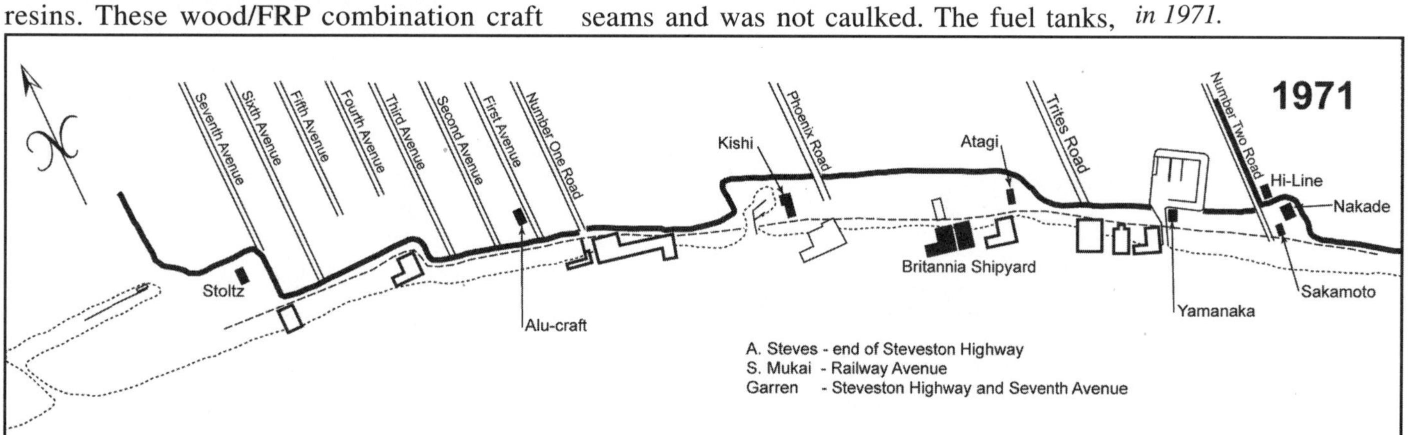

*Bob Karliner's **ELSIE K No. II** ready for launching on the Stoltz Brothers Boat Works ways. (1955)(B. Karliner collection)*

water tanks, mast and net rollers for this vessel were made of steel. The cabin and deck were built of plywood and covered with FRP.

There was also a demand for larger, faster and maintenance-free vessels. The Stoltz Brothers Boat Works constructed Bob Karliner's ***ELSIE K No II*** in 1955. This vessel was designed by Robert Allan, and had a 37-foot length, a 10-foot 4-inch beam, a 3-foot 7-inch depth, and was powered by a V-8, 250 HP Chrysler gasoline engine. The vessel cost $12,300.

This boat works was the first to build a solid FRP fishing vessel in Steveston in 1961. This vessel, the ***HAPPY TIME IV***, was designed by John Brandlmayer and cost

*Yonni Sakai's **HAPPY TIME IV**, the first fibreglass reinforced plastic (FRP) fishing boat constructed in Steveston. (ca. 1963)(Y. Sakai collection)*

Ed Kowalski's ***SOLAN*** *built by the Shore Boat Works in 1968. This boat was powered by a 6-cylinder, 125 HP International engine. (1971)(MY)*

$18,000. It had a 36-foot 11-inch length, a 10-foot 4-inch beam, a 3-foot 8-inch depth, and was powered by a V-8, 280 HP Chrysler gasoline engine. FRP became the preferred material for small fishing boat construction in the early 1970s.

TRITES MARINE started fabricating aluminum skiffs in the early 1970s for the roe herring fishery. ALU-CRAFT built power-skiffs for BC Packers, and gillnetters for the Skeena River and Bristol Bay fisheries. Aluminum boats were generally more costly to build than those made with FRP, but their popularity increased because they were light, fast, and easy to maintain.

Fishing Nets.

About 1952 a few fishermen purchased nets woven of synthetic twine from Vancouver Nylon Nets. These nets were so superior that most fishermen had purchased them by the following salmon season. The nylon nets were stronger, less absorbent and easier to haul than linen nets. Their synthetic fibre did not require periodic drying and bluestone treatment, and bluestone tanks became obsolete by the mid 1950s.

Wharves

There was a complete renovation of the Steveston waterfront in the early 1950s. Fishing companies replanked wharves and fortified the pilings. They also enlarged wharves and built new ones. The companies, especially BC Packers, also constructed new net floats for their fishermen.

Each net float could hold four racked nets, and was usually shared by four gillnet fishermen. Bluestone tanks were set under the decking at the four corners of the float. When the fishermen returned to their moorages at a net float after the Saturday eight o'clock morning closure, they worked together to pull the gillnets off the drums, and to string them onto the net racks. Then each fisherman washed his net, mended the holes, and pulled the gillnet off the net rack for treatment with a copper sulfate solution in his bluestone tank. Then he rolled the net from the tank onto the drum ready for the eight o'clock Monday morning opening. He threw a burlap cover over the net, so the sunshine would not react with the chemical preservative and weaken the linen webbing. After nylon nets were introduced, the fishermen rolled the nets directly onto the drum after repairing any damage.

To supply more safe moorage for fishing boats the Canadian Fishing Company dredged Scotch Pond in 1952 and Nelson Brothers Fishing Company dredged their boat basin in 1962.

By the late 1960s fishermen were concerned that there was little independent moorage. Fishermen who tied up at company

Paramount Pond, owned by Nelson Brothers Fisheries, was dredged in 1962 to provide moorage for the increasing numbers of larger fishing vessels. (1971)(MY)

Net floats at the Canadian Pacific camp. The largest numbers of net floats were used on the Steveston waterfront during this interval. (1971)(MY)

wharves were expected to fish for the companies, but cash buyers paid more for fish. Stradiotti, a cash buyer, had a barge at the foot of Seventh Avenue, and many fishermen sold part of their catches at this barge.

In 1967 the Steveston Community Society set up the Steveston Waterfront Task Force to campaign for independent moorage and a fishermen's wharf where fish could be sold directly to the public. Harold Steves Sr. directed this campaign, and the committee included Buck Suzuki for the UFAWU, Brian Fraser for the Fisheries Association, and various other Steveston representatives.

Federal Fisheries Minister Jack Davis agreed to the proposal, and initiated several studies, which recommended new independent moorage and a major unloading facility for fresh and frozen fish. In 1974 the small Craft Harbours Branch of the federal government proposed plans for a fishboat harbour costing $20,000,000 on the west end of Steveston Island.

The need for independent moorage grew after BC Packers bought out the other Steveston canneries, and many canneries, wharves, floats, boat lifts and net lofts were allowed to deteriorate.

Fishermen mending nets during the weekend closure. (ca. 1953)(MY)

Fishing Activities

The 1950s was a decade of unprecedented diversification. Fishermen were forced to explore alternative fisheries and fishing grounds because of increased competition from larger improved boats and superior nylon nets.

Some fishermen never left the Fraser River. They started gillnetting for early spring salmon in March or April, sockeyes in July, pinks (during odd-numbered years), fall springs and cohos in September, and chums in October.

West Coast Trolling

In the spring of 1951 Yoshiaki Murao on the ***HARLOCK***, Kasuichi Sakai on the

LILLIAN, Kumataro Sakiyama on the ***CAPE BELLE*** and Ichiro Shiho on the ***RIO SENORITA*** rigged their gillnetters with trolling poles and gurdies and departed for Barclay Sound. They trolled the west coast of Vancouver Island for spring and coho salmon until August. When they returned to Steveston, they replaced the trolling gear with net drums and rollers and gillnetted for late sockeyes, pinks, cohos and chums. In the following year seven more fishermen rigged their boats for combination trolling and gillnetting, and many more followed in the ensuing years.

Miyakichi Yesaki's ***WILD WEST*** *was built by Nakade Boat Works in the summer of 1952 for $9,000. The engine in this vessel was a gasoline 6-cylinder, 115 HP Nordberg .Yesaki rigged the vessel to troll and gillnet for salmon during the 1953 season. (1953)(MY)*

Straits of Juan de Fuca Gillnetting

From 1946 to 1953 a few gillnetters fished the Straits of Juan de Fuca (Area 20), trying to intercept the Adams River and other sockeye salmon runs. Catches for these years ranged from 1,900 to 4,700 sockeyes. During the Adams River cycle year of 1954, Harry Thompson fished out of San Juan on his ***HEATHER MAY*** with a 250 fathom net. At first about twelve gillnetters from the New Westminster area were fishing off San Juan, but rumours of large catches soon attracted many more fishermen. Gillnetters captured 87,000 sockeye salmon in the Straits of Juan de Fuca that year. This area became a significant fishing ground in subsequent years.

In 1955 there were no boundaries and gear restrictions for the Straits of Juan de Fuca, so Bob Karliner with his new vessel ***ELSIE K No. II*** fished a gillnet 750 fathoms long and 150 meshes deep. He occasionally caught 1,000 salmon in a night's operation. However,

A night's catch of dogfish in the Straits of Juan de Fuca off San Juan. (1955)(B. Karliner collection)

dogfish sometimes invaded the fishing grounds and raised havoc with the nets. In 1957 gillnetting was prohibited offshore of the "blue-line" from Bonilla Point, British Columbia to Tatoosh Island, Washington. Net size was limited to 300 fathoms in length and 90 meshes in depth.

Shrimp Beam Trawling

In the fall of 1951 Japanese fishermen at the Canadian Pacific Camp and the Gulf of Georgia Cannery began experimenting with gillnet drums to set and haul beam trawls for catching shrimp. They wanted a fill-in fishery for the period from December to March.

The Canadian Pacific Camp fishermen included Hideo Maeda on the ***SHELAINE***, Eiji Maeda on the ***WEST WIND***, Toshiyuki Sameshima on the ***SALMON QUEEN***, Eizo Sameshima on the ***EVENING STAR***, Toshiharu Sameshima on the ***LARI-ANN***, Toshio Sameshima on the ***VICKY MAY*** and Matsuo Matsumura on the ***LOYAL LADY***. The fishermen on each boat used a 4-inch by 4-inch, 40-foot fir timber for the beam and three-quarter inch manila rope for the warp. They fashioned the trawl with herring webbing from a design obtained from Japan. They used the drum to retrieve, store and set the warp and the trawl, and to haul the beam over the stern and the entire length of the vessel. They stored the beam on a cross-tree on the mast, with one end high over the bow and the other end on the stern.

A fisherman hauling shrimp trawl and a galvanized steel beam with a gillnet drum. (1971)(MY)

The wooden beam became water-logged and lost its buoyancy after a day's fishing because of the water pressure at 30 to 50 fathom depths. To counter this, the fishermen tied glass balls onto the beam. They also carried two beams, and fished them on alternate days to let them dry out. They left a third beam drying at Canadian Pacific Camp, and replaced one beam each week. Hideo and Eiji Maeda had a friend who worked at Wilkinson Steel. About 1955 this friend suggested replacing the wooden beams with steel tubing. They welded two 4-inch diameter, 21-foot sections of galvanized tubing together into a 42-foot beam, and capped this beam at the ends. The steel beam fished as well as the wooden beam, and did not become water-logged. The use of the gillnet drum and the steel beam greatly increased the efficiency of beam trawling.

The Canadian Pacific Camp fishermen generally fished in the Gulf Islands off Chemainus, Ladysmith and False Narrows. The fishermen in each boat started at daybreak, trawled for three hours, then hauled the net. They made another set, and sorted the shrimp catch while trawling for three more hours. They returned to their anchorage for the night, and sorted the catch of the last set before dark. Two designated carrier boats delivered the catches to Steveston by 8 o'clock the following morning, unloaded and returned that day to the fishing grounds. Two other vessels were designated to transport that day's catches to Steveston.

The two groups of fishermen eventually formed co-operatives to process their shrimp catches. The Gulf of Georgia group built a "shrimp factory" at Chatham Street and Seventh Avenue near Garry Point. BC Packers permitted the Canadian Pacific group to use

the Imperial Cannery processing facilities, and also marketed their product. After the catches were delivered to the Imperial Cannery by the two carrier boats, workers immediately cooked the shrimp in vats, then cooled and peeled the shrimp. The shrimpers fished daily from Sunday through Thursday to ensure daily shrimp deliveries from Monday through Friday. By the early 1960s up to thirty vessels were participating in the Canadian Pacific co-operative. The members of this co-operative stopped processing their catches in the Imperial Cannery in 1964.

Sockeye Salmon Troll Fishery

The troll fishery traditionally captured only spring and coho salmon. Most people thought that sockeye, pink and chum would not take troll lures because these salmon fed on plankton. However, this did not discourage troll fishermen up and down the coast from trying to catch these species.

Hideo (Henry) Kokubo tried lures made from Leckie hootchies and cod skin strips while fishing out of Nanaimo in 1954. Nagasaki, a Japanese scientist on a short study tour at the Pacific Biological Station, told Kokubo of Japanese experiments with similar artificial lures for their salmon longlines. Later Kokubo's younger brother Masaya visited Nagasaki in Japan, and got 6 experimental hootchies from the Yamashita Fishing Tackle Factory. These were only about 2 inches long, so Kukubo mixed strands from these hootchies with those of the longer Leckie hootchies. Catches with these lures were encouraging. The following winter, Masaya Kokubo ordered two dozen each of five different coloured

An 8 o'clock Monday morning set in the Albion, with the rock jetty extension of Albion Dyke No. 1 and North Jetty in the background. (ca. 1958)(MY)

hootchies. He also advised Yamashita to make hootchies with finer and longer strands and of different colours. Masaya on the west coast and Henry in Silva Bay both had good catches with these lures.

Henry Kokubo contracted Sakamoto Boatworks to build his ***ELMA K*** in 1958. The boat was rigged with a fixed gillnet drum and trolling gurdies so that a change-over of fishing gear could be completed in a few hours. On earlier combination gillnet/troll vessels, gillnet gear had to be removed before troll gear was installed.

In the early autumn of 1959, Henry Kokubo was gillnetting sockeyes and pinks on the Fraser River. Gillnetters were allowed two days fishing, and then there was a five-day closure before the next opening. Kokubo asked Tom Rothery, the Fishery Inspector at that time, if there were any restrictions on trolling during the gillnet closure. Rothery confirmed there were no restrictions, so Kokubo went out the next day and trolled single flashers with hootchies outside the Sandheads, and caught 19 fish. The following day, he trolled from Sand Heads to Point Grey, and caught two dozen fish. Next morning, he trolled from Point Grey to Sand Heads and got into a school of fish. He caught 2,000 pounds of sockeyes and pinks during the three days. Other fishermen with combination gillnet/troll vessels soon started trolling off the mouth of the Fraser River during the gillnet closure.

The "mosquito fleet" tied to the Albion Dyke No. 1 waiting for the tide. (ca. 1954)(MY)

Pacific Salmon Commission records for the Straits of Georgia off the Fraser River showed no sockeye catches by trolling gear up to 1960. Trollers captured 2,800 sockeyes in this area in 1961. The International Salmon Fisheries Commission enacted regulations in 1962 and the following years prohibiting fishing with troll gear for sockeyes and pinks from late summer to early fall off the mouth of the Fraser River. In more recent years, Gulf trollers have been allowed to troll for sockeye and pink salmon in this area during gillnet openings.

Pacific Salmon Commission statistics for Canadian waters showed the sockeye landings with troll gear ranged between 400 and 24,300 from 1954 to 1959. These were incidental captures while fishing for springs and cohos off the west coast. However, a few fishermen were targeting sockeye salmon with pink hootchie lures from Yamashita Fishing Tackle off the west coast in 1959 when the 24,300 fish were caught. The troll catch of sockeye increased to 21,700 in 1966 and exploded to 161,800 in 1967, when the west coast troll fleet started targeting sockeye salmon. Thereafter, sockeye catches by trolling gear exceeded 30,000 fish in all but two of the seventeen years to 1984.

"Mosquito Fleet"

Boys have probably gillnetted with rowboats since the commercial salmon fishery began on the Fraser River. Buck Suzuki started fishing at nine years old with a rowboat off Don Island. Bob Karliner fished the North Arm when he was thirteen. Harry Thompson started with a skiff out of Steveston at twelve years old. In 1952 Joji Yamanaka, Mitsuo Yesaki, Satoshi Hamada, Mitsuo Teraguchi and Walter Tokai started fishing out of Steveston with flat-bottom skiffs powered with outboard motors. The skiffs ranged in length from 12 to 15 feet, and the motors from 3 HP to 25 HP. They fished gillnets 150 fathoms long and 30 meshes deep. These skiffs were efficient fishing units because of the low capital investment, high speed and easy access to shallow fishing grounds. The "mosquito fleet" fished primarily in the Albion and the south arm flats. The

A Japanese women doing the laundry outside a Pacific Coast Cannery house. (1951) (MY)

original skiffs were soon joined by many others. The numbers of "mosquito" skiffs peaked in the early 1960s. Some of the "mosquito" fishermen took up permanent jobs on shore, and others graduated to larger boats.

Fishermen

During the war Japanese was spoken in the households of Issei and older Nisei, where the children learned enough Japanese to communicate with their parents. Children of younger Nisei and Sansei spoke only English, and many Japanese lost their language. The Japanese Canadians also lost their social and political ties with Japan. After gaining citizenship in June 1948 the Japanese were totally committed to integrating into Canadian society and building their life in Canada. They retained only familial ties and a modicum of cultural ties with their ancestral land.

In April 1953 Prince Akihito made an official stop in Vancouver en route to London for the coronation of Queen Elizabeth II. Japanese students of Richmond High School were given permission to take a schoool day off to meet the Prince. A group of boys from grade ten and eleven rode the tram into downtown Vancouver, took in a matinee at one of the theatres on Granville Street, then boarded a bus to "China town" for a Chinese meal before returning to Steveston. The Vancouver Sun reported a cheering crowd of 100 Japanese Canadians waving Canadian and Japanese flags as the Prince disembarked from the plane.

Cannery Houses

A few of the returning Japanese fishermen purchased homes while others rented available houses. In January 1950 the fishing companies started renting their cannery houses to Japanese. Three fishermen moved into one of the BC Packers cannery houses at Pacific Coast camp and stayed there until they moved aboard their newly acquired boats. In March and April 1950 Japanese families moved into the Pacific Coast Camp cannery houses and the BC Packers cannery houses at the Imperial Cannery. Nelson Brothers Fisheries offered the cannery houses at Colonial Camp to their fishermen. The largest number of Japanese families was accommodated in the Gulf of

Gulf of Georgia cannery houses where many Japanese families stayed after returning to the coast. (1971)(MY)

Georgia cannery houses belonging to the Canadian Fishing Company. The ABC Company moved five cannery houses to the west side of Trites Road for their Japanese fishermen. Great West Packing constructed four new houses along Trites Road and six new houses on Andrews Road.

The one storey and one-and-a-half storey cannery houses at the Pacific Coast camp had not changed from 1900 to 1950, except for the addition of shingle siding and the oil-fired kitchen stoves. This cluster of houses connected by boardwalks was built entirely on pilings. The inside walls were covered with shiplap with no insulation between the studs. The floors in the living room and bedrooms were made of tongue-and-groove flooring, and the kitchen floor was covered with linoleum. Heat was provided by a wood-fired sheet metal stove and the oil burner in the kitchen stove. Hot water for the kitchen sink was heated by a coil of copper tubing in the oil burner and stored in a steel tank. The only water faucets in the house were at the kitchen sink and by the outside washroom.

Japanese fishermen started leaving the cannery houses in the early 1950s after buying properties and building new homes. The last Japanese family in a Pacific Coast cannery house left it in the early 1970s. In 1977 the municipality decreed all residences in Steveston had to be connected to the sewage system. Almost all of the remaining cannery houses on the Steveston waterfront were demolished after this ruling.

The boardwalk and one-storey cannery houses at the Pacific Coast camp. The bicycles were the principal mode of travel for children on the waterfront. The children were constantly afraid that the front wheels would fall into the cracks between the boards and they would be flipped off. (ca. 1951)(MY)

The Years of Decline

Chapter

8

1975 - 1997

Main Channel of the Fraser River

In 1991 the federal government began to reconstruct a one-mile long training wall at Steveston Bend between the harbour and the Sand Heads. This wall would keep a 35-foot deep channel free from silt. It cost $16,000,000.

A geological study released in May 1992 found the 38-year old Sand Heads Lighthouse at risk of being swept into the sea as unstable sediment on the ocean floor shifted. Three lightkeepers there were reassigned to other lighthouses on the British Columbia coast. In December 1993 the Canadian Coast Guard recommended that Sand Heads be permanantly automated, despite protests by commercial fishermen, the United Fishermen and Allied Workers Union, recreational boaters, mariners, pilots and even Richmond City Council. In February 1996 the BC Government investigated restaffing the Sand Heads lighthouse.

Townsite and Waterfront

During this period Richmond changed from a bedroom community for Vancouver to a satellite civic centre with many shopping malls. Rising property values shifted construction from single-family units to multi-family townhouses and high-rise apartments. Immigrants from Hong Kong, Taiwan and other Asian countries settled in Richmond. By 1995 over 30 percent of the population was comprised of people with Chinese ancestry. In 1980 three apartments called Fraser Place were built west of Steveston facing Garry Point. The City of Richmond purchased Garry Point in 1981 and changed its use from sand storage to waterfront park, after concerned citizens won a legal court battle to prevent high-rises on the property. By 1995 the residential area within half a mile of the Steveston business district had more townhouses and apartment units than single family units. Large multi-family buildings had also been built along the waterfront north of the Paramount Pond and Britannia Shipyard.

The number of businesses in Steveston began to increase in the 1980s and gained momentum in the 1990s. The earlier additions were mainly businesses serving residents in the southwest corner of Lulu Island. The later additions, including the Steveston Landing complex built on the original Steves Landing or "City Wharf" site at the foot of Second Avenue in 1988, provided consumer goods and services for increasing numbers of visitors to Steveston.

The economic base of the town changed during this period from exclusively fishing to a combination of fishing and tourism. The major attraction was the unique waterfront with an active fishing industry, and a colourful weekend market of fishermen selling their catches directly to the public. Other attractions included the historic sites of the Gulf of

Steveston Landing was developed by the federal government in 1988 on the Star, Steveston and Lighthouse sites. The wharf was restricted to fishing boats selling fish directly to the public and to tour boats. (1995)(MY)

Townhouses encroaching on the Steveston waterfront beside the Britannia Shipyard Historic Site. (1997)(MY)

The Gulf of Georgia site purchased by the federal government in 1977. The Gulf of Georgia Cannery Society operated a display centre in part of the complex, and the Canadian Fishing Company leased the remainder for net and gear storage for its seine and gillnet fleet. (1997)(MY)

Georgia Cannery and the Britannia Shipyard, and the trail system on the dike along the Sturgeon Bank flats and South Arm of the Fraser River.

Lord Byng School

In 1993 Richmond Council and Richmond School Board paid $100,000 to move the 1925 four-room Lord Byng School to a temporary site. They intended to restore it permanently on the site of the 1947 fourteen-room building. This would have commemorated the co-operation of the Japanese parents who paid for half the "Little School" or Annex in 1925, so their children could attend. A new one-level Lord Byng School opened in October 1995, and the parents demanded playing fields, not heritage buildings. A new council turned down proposals by a music school and a Chinese cultural centre to lease and repair the Little School and both of the original buildings were demolished in 1996. The new school board developed a Japanese rock garden to honour Hideko Hyodo, the pre-war Lord Byng teacher who organized the education in the internment camps during the war.

Development of the Commercial Fishery

About 1,000 vessels fished on the Fraser River between 1975 and 1995. The average number of fishing days per week during the entire sockeye season on the Fraser River declined from 1.9 to 1.0 days. Strict restrictions were needed because of the increasing efficiency of the fishing gear and vessels, and the higher interception of fish outside the traditional gillnet fishing grounds.

In 1995 the government raised the price of commercial fishing licenses from $800 to $1,390 for a gillnet license, from $1,600 to $5,750 for a salmon seine license, and from $20 to $990 for a Native Indian gillnet license. Fishermen needed separate licenses for each area they fished, and each gear type they used (seine, gillnet, troll). License stacking (holding two or more licenses) became common.

In 1995 and 1996 the federal Department of Fisheries and Oceans under Minister Fred Mifflin bought out 800 salmon licenses at a cost of $72.2 million to reduce the commercial fleet in British Columbia to 3,300 vessels. The government allotted $36 million in 1996 to retrain commercial fishermen in new job skills.

The number of fishing days for other

salmon species was also markedly reduced. In the early 1950s fishing for spring, pink, coho and chum was permitted five days a week. By 1995 the Fraser River stocks of spring and coho salmon were at historic low levels. Fishing was not permitted for spring salmon, except during occasional openings for Native fishermen. Fishing for pinks and chums was restricted to one and two day openings during the autumn.

The long-standing problem of Aboriginal fishing rights was resolved in the Supreme Court of Canada. In May 1990 in a landmark case involving Ron Sparrow of the Musqueam Band the Court ruled that the Native food fishery had precedence over the commercial and sports fisheries after conservation measures had been met. In July 1991 Fisheries Minister John Crosbie established a separate Aboriginal Fishery. The Fraser River became the scene of clashes between Native and Commercial fishermen when openings for Native fishermen preceded openings for other fishermen. The Native catch increased to 874,000 fish. Under the Aboriginal Fisheries Strategy a new Lower Fraser Fishing Authority, comprised of the Musqueam, Tsawwassen and Sto:lo Bands, was permitted to sell 395,000 sockeye salmon. However, in August 1996 the Supreme Court ruled that an Indian band had a right to catch fish to sell only if it could establish that selling fish was an integral part of its culture prior to contact with Europeans. Thus the Sto:lo did not have the right to sell salmon, but the Teiltsukl had the right to sell herring roe.

The runs of the Fraser River sockeye salmon continued to increase during this period under the stewardship of the International Pacific Salmon Commission and the Pacific Salmon Commission. The sockeye catches from 1975 to 1995 averaged 11.7 million fish in dominant years, and 6.4 million in off-years. The Canadian commercial fishermen's share averaged 71 percent, with the American fishermen taking 22 percent and the Canadian Native fishermen 7 percent.

Limited Licenses

Limited licenses and the buy-back program introduced in 1968 lowered the number of salmon fishing vessels, but not their fishing power. With shorter salmon fishing seasons, fishermen increased their efforts to catch other species during the off-season. These fisheries in turn were soon plagued with excessive fishing, requiring stringent regulatory measures. Licenses in the lucrative roe herring fishery were limited in 1974 to previous year participants. Limited licensing was introduced for bottomfish in 1976, followed by abalone and shrimp in 1977 and halibut in 1979. By the early 1990s, almost all the commercial fisheries on the British Columbia coast were regulated by limited licensing.

Limited license fisheries were generally regulated by catch quotas. This encouraged a gold-rush mentality in fishermen to catch as much as possible in the shortest time to obtain a higher proportion of the quota. The results were usually market gluts and low prices during the fishing season, and market shortages and high prices during closures.

In the 1990s an Individual Vessel Quota (IVQ) system was introduced into the halibut, geoduck and blackcod fisheries. Each vessel was given a specified quota, which could be taken at any time during the year. This system encouraged fishermen to plan their trips to off-

Map of Steveston waterfront showing locations of canneries in 1995. (clear building - non-operating)

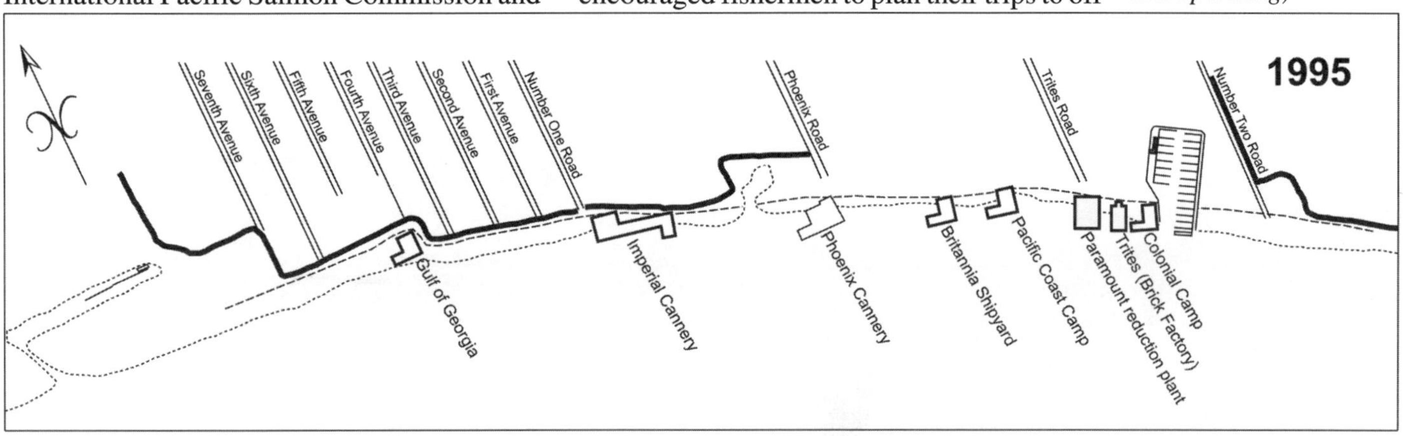

load catches when prices were highest, during periods of good weather, and around openings for other fisheries.

Canneries and Other Waterfront Enterprises

The New England Fishing Company had financial difficulties in Eastern USA, and sold the Gulf of Georgia Cannery to the federal government in 1977. A new CanFisCo operation under Jimmy Pattison continued canning and processing fish in the Home Plant in Vancouver. The Gulf of Georgia herring reduction plant was operated until 1979. By 1975 BC Packers had become the principal fish processor and private landowner on the Steveston waterfront. In 1980 the company bought the Oceanside Cannery near Prince Rupert from CanFisCo, and began to rebuild and concentrate its canning operations in this newer plant.

Salmon canning at the Imperial Plant became less important than the year-round bottomfish operations, processing mainly frozen products. Then the General Agreement on Tariffs and Trade (GATT) allowed up to 20 percent of fish caught in Canada in 1990 to be processed in the United States. This percentage was increased to 25 percent in 1991. BC Packers began directing a large portion of its groundfish to a plant in Anacortes, Washington, also owned by George Weston Limited.

In 1990 during the largest Fraser River sockeye run since the Hell's Gate disaster (21 million fish), the BC Packers plants at Steveston and Prince Rupert together processed 2.2 million pounds of fish daily. During the five weeks of fishing, 800 cannery workers processed fish at the Imperial plant.

The demand for frozen spring, sockeye, coho, pink and chum salmon had expanded with improved freezing technologies, better distribution systems and new markets. Exports of frozen sockeye salmon to Japan surged after the 200 mile Exclusive Economic Zone was established in the early 1970s, and Japanese high seas salmon gillnetters were banned from the eastern North Pacific Ocean. Salted sockeye salmon sides had been exported to Japan since the 1980s. Frozen pink and chum salmon had been retailed through the major supermarket chains in North America. A specialized high-end market for smoked salmon grew with the recent boom in tourism in British Columbia. These alternative markets for salmon greatly reduced the quantity of raw material used for canning. Fisheries Statistics of Canada showed canned salmon accounted for only 47 percent of the total landings in 1993, down from 60 percent in 1984 and 80 percent in 1955. Of the other 53 percent, 38 percent was marketed as frozen fish, 11 percent as fresh fish and 4 percent as smoked or salted fish.

A significant proportion of the fresh, frozen, smoked and salted salmon for specialty markets was processed by many small plants built since the 1970s. The only plant in Steveston was built by S. Matsuo and Sons on the Nakade boat works site at the foot of Number Two Road in 1973. *Suzuko*, *kazunoko*, smoked and salted salmon were processed at this plant. It was taken over by Kawaki Canada

The Phoenix site purchased by BC Packers in 1969. The cannery was shut down, except for the ice plant, and was partially destroyed by fire in 1997. (1995)(MY)

BC Packers stopped canning salmon at the Imperial Cannery in 1992, and closed all operations in late 1996. (1997)(MY)

in 1992.

In 1991 BC Packers transferred its farmed salmon processing operations from the Imperial Plant to Brown's Bay Packing, a non-union plant north of Campbell River, which was closer to its fish farms. In November 1992 after 100 years of continuous operation, the Imperial Plant stopped canning fish, and concentrated on fresh fish products. *Kazunoko*, a high-priced herring roe product with a unique market in Japan, was processed at the Imperial plant until 1996.

In 1993 BC Packers and its major competitor CanFisCo co-operated to build a cannery at Ketchikan in Alaska. In August 1996 BC Packers amalgamated with CanFisCo to form Allied Pacific Processors. They closed the Imperial Plant and transferred all their herring and salmon operations from Steveston to CanFisCo's Home Plant in Vancouver.

The Imperial Plant had not been operating at full capacity since 1990. Financial returns from fish processing were declining, while the residential value of waterfront properties was sky-rocketing. BC Packers had already sold large tracts of waterfront property to residential developers. The company had concluded it was more profitable to consolidate fish processing operations away from Steveston, and began negotiations with the City of Richmond to rezone the remaining forty acres of Imperial and Phoenix properties for residential and commercial development.

Salmon Farming

In the early 1970s entrepreneurs started farming Pacific spring and coho salmon along British Columbia's Sunshine Coast. By 1985 there were seventeen operating fish farms in British Columbia. After the Conservative Government repealed the Foreign Investment Act, and the Department of Fisheries and Oceans permitted the importation of Atlantic salmon roe for cultivation in 1984, foreign capital flooded into the fledgling fish farming industry. Young Atlantic salmon were more difficult to culture, but grew twice as fast as Pacific spring and coho when transferred to salt water.

By 1989 there were about eighty local companies operating 185 small farms on the entire coast, with a total production of 12,500 tons. However, prices collapsed because of global overproduction of farmed salmon and large catches of wild salmon in 1990. Most of the companies, under-funded and relying primarily on credit for operations, were forced into bankruptcy. A massive consolidation left seventeen companies operating eighty farms by 1993. The salmon farming industry was completely transformed into a multi-national agri-business run by corporations with secure financial resources. By 1995 Atlantic salmon accounted for 70 percent of the production from British Columbia salmon farms.

In 1996 more than 50 of the 105 salmon

The Kawaki Canada plant processed smoked and salted salmon for export to Japan. (1995) (MY)

The Britannia Shipyard site was purchased from BC Packers by the municipal government in 1989. The Britannia Heritage Shipyard Society was registered in 1991 to preserve the site. (1995)(MY)

The Pacific Coast site was purchased by the federal government. In December 1997, the cannery building was demolished by the Steveston Harbour Authority, which operated harbours for small commercial boats upstream and downstream of the building. (1995)(MY)

farms in British Columbia were owned and operated by three groups: Norwegian Stolt Sea Farms, BC Packers, and the Omega Salmon Group, an amalgamation of Norwegian firms.

The catch of wild salmon in British Columbia for 1995 was 48,000 metric tons. The production of farmed salmon in 1995 was 24,000 metric tons for British Columbia and 613,000 metric tons for the world. The salmon farming industry was able to provide traditional markets seeking fresh and frozen salmon with a steady year-round supply of premium quality fresh fish.

Fishing Heritage Preservation

Two major heritage sites preserved during this period were the Gulf of Georgia Cannery and the Britannia Heritage Shipyard. The Canadian Parks Service acquired the Gulf of Georgia Cannery building in 1984, and with the help of the Gulf of Georgia Cannery Society developed historical displays and a small theatre to depict the west coast fishing industry. In 1990 the City of Richmond was given 8.4 acres of the Britannia Shipyard when BC Packers sold the property to a developer. The City and the Britannia Heritage Shipyard Society together developed the site for an operating shipyard and a marine centre.

Boatworks

The last wooden boatworks in Steveston, Kishi Boat Works, closed in 1985. The last wooden fishing boat built on the Steveston waterfront was the ***MICKLEY***. This boat was 40.6 feet in length, 15.2 feet in breadth, 6.9 feet in depth, and was powered by a 237 HP diesel engine. Bill Sigurgeirson and Doreen Joliff and several members of their families built this

vessel in a temporary shed behind the industrial park on Trites Road in 1990. Sigurgeirson followed the traditional method of designing a vessel by taking lines off a three-foot half model carved out of wood. Kris Frostad supervised the project and put in the oak ribs and the fir planking, and Raymond Bardnes did the caulking. Sigurgeirson and Joliff planned to use the vessel for trolling salmon and tuna, and longlining rockfish.

The Stoltz Boat Works stopped operating in 1977. The Yamanaka Boat Works moved its operations to Delta in 1979. The D.M. Garren Boat Works at Steveston Highway and Seventh Avenue built foam-core FRP boats until 1978, but few were fishing boats. SI-PORT Industries, the last FRP boat works in Steveston, started building boats in 1992 and closed in 1996.

Fishing vessels constructed of marine-grade aluminum became more popular after the early 1970s because of their lightweight and low maintenance. Kurt Csontala operated ALU-CRAFT, the first aluminum boat works in Steveston, at several locations in Steveston between 1971 and 1987. Bob Gordon started HI-LINE Aluminum Welding in 1976, and moved his operation into a new building at the foot of Number Two Road in 1978. Eldon and Rick Thompson formed THOMPSON BROS. Aluminum Welding near Annacis Island in 1985 and moved their operation to First Avenue south of Moncton Street in Steveston about 1990. KIMURA Welding was started in 1987 and closed in 1996. Jerry Takahashi started the NU BOAT marine boat works in 1992, building and modifying boats in a warehouse on Trites Road. MILOUSH Advanced Mobile Welding was transferred to a building near TRITES MARINE in 1992. ACTION Welding Services was relocated to a building on Second Avenue in 1996.

*The **SANDY ISLE** was built for David Kadyschuck by Thompson Bros. in 1994 for about $150,000. This vessel was 42 feet long and one of the largest super punts. It was rigged for gillnetting salmon with the cabin module. (1995)(MY)*

Fishing Boats

Two basic types of small fishing vessels were built during the 1970s and 1980s. The displacement hull vessels were approximately 38 feet long and could cruise at about 10 mph.

Map of the Steveston waterfront showing locations of boat works in 1995.

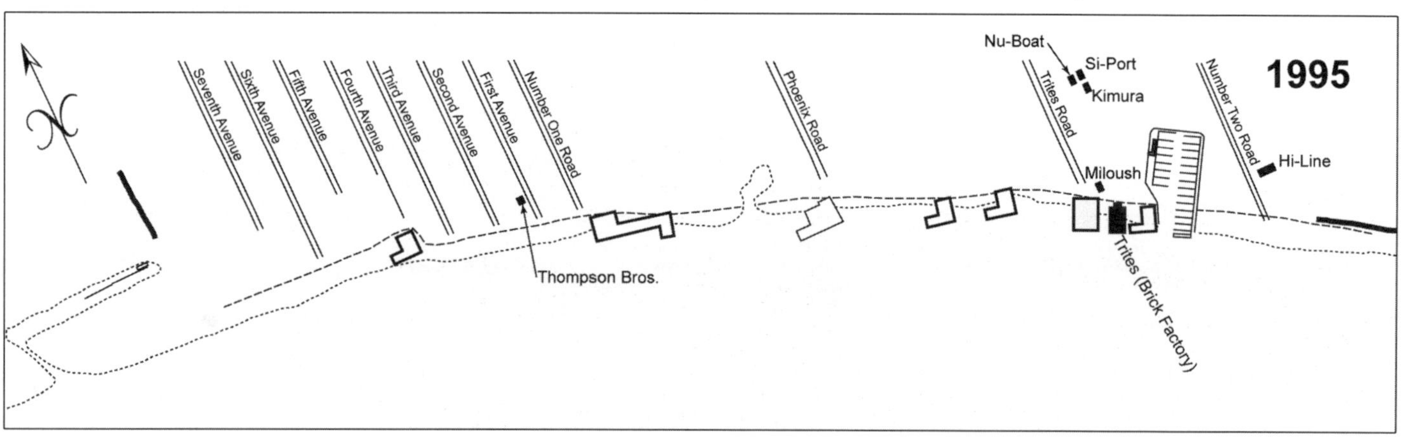

They were used mainly for gillnetting and trolling salmon and longlining halibut, but also for beam-trawling shrimp and longlining rockfish in the off-season. The planing hull vessels had either conventional propeller/shaft systems or inboard/outboard drives. They were about 30 feet long, and cruised at 15 to 25 mph. They were used almost exclusively in gillnetting for salmon from the stern or bow. The bowpicker was first used in the Columbia River fishery.

Prices for roe herring soared in the 1980s and early 1990s. Roe herring from British Columbia commanded the highest prices because of its superior quality. Premium prices were paid for roe herring caught by gillnetters because of higher yields. This was an extremely lucrative fishery and fishermen could make fortunes in a single day. When the roe fishery started in 1972, herring gillnets were set and hauled manually from aluminum punts powered by outboard motors. Later, powered rollers and shakers were used to set and haul the gillnets and shake the fish off the nets. A salmon fisherman with a herring license generally had a salmon gillnetter and a herring punt. As herring punts and outboard motors increased in size, and equipment became more complex, rising costs prompted development of the super punt, a combination vessel for gillnetting salmon and herring.

The earliest super punt, the ***ABRACADABRA***, was built for Roger Obayashi by THOMPSON BROS. in 1988. This planing hull vessel was 33.9 feet in length. It was powered by an inboard Volvo diesel engine coupled to an outboard drive, and cruised at 20 mph. A removable cabin module was attached to an extended deck forward of the gillnet drum bulkhead. Insulated plastic totes were carried between the cabin and gillnet drum for salmon gillnetting. The cabin module and totes were removed for herring gillnetting. A net roller and a shaker were attached on the gunwales and rectangular hoop nets were set in the extended deck to collect the catch.

Two later superpunts were Paul Kershaw's ***JET-LAG I*** and Terry Taylor's ***JUST TRAVELLIN***, built in 1992 by THOMPSON BROS. These planing hull vessels were 39.4 feet in length, 12 feet in breadth, 4.7 feet in depth, and were powered by twin 300 HP Volvo diesels coupled to Hamilton Jet drives. They had extended forward decks with rollers and shakers on the gunwales, and gillnet drums on the sterns. They attained speeds of 38 mph during trials. The ***JUST TRAVELLIN*** was fitted with a forward cabin module and four insulated plastic totes mid-ship for salmon gillnetting.

Wharves

The number of fish processors increased noticeably during the 1970s as new markets were developed. These processors were able to pay fishermen higher prices than fishing companies because they did not have to

The Colonial site was purchased by the federal government. The cannery building was used for net and gear storage by gillnet fishermen. (1995)(MY)

The Paramount site was purchased by the federal government and leased by BC Packers for net and gear storage for its seine fleet. (1997)(MY)

provide facilities and services to fishermen. Moreover, as fishermen became independent of the fishing companies, they could sell their catches to cash buyers without fear of retaliation if they had alternate places to moor their boats. The fishing companies were also anxious to reduce their commitments to maintenance of fishermen's facilities. Steveston fishermen petitioned for a public wharf with a fresh fish market. However, many people worried that the federal proposal for moorage on Steveston Island would cause environmental damage, and that fishing services and supplies would have to be relocated.

In 1975 Bud Sakamoto, a Steveston architect and part-time fisherman, and Harold Steves, provincial MLA for Richmond from 1972 to 1975, suggested the provincial government co-operate with the federal government to buy CanFisCo's Gulf of Georgia site, valued at $2,000,000 for seven acres. The federal government bought this waterfront land in 1977, leased the building back to CanFisCo for net and gear storage, and developed a floating quay for large boats.

The Paramount Cannery site was purchased by the federal government and leased by BC Packers for an ice plant and net and gear storage for its seine fleet. The Colonial site was also purchased by the federal government, and used for net and gear storage by gillnet fishermen. The Small Craft Harbours Branch of the Department of Fisheries and Oceans completed major repairs on their facilities for gillnetters and seiners. In 1989

Scotch Pond with net floats and fishing vessels. This is the only remaining harbour where fishermen were assigned net floats for mooring their vessels and repairing their nets. (1995)(MY)

the Steveston Harbour Authority took over the management of all the fishing vessel facilities except the remaining BC Packers waterfront, and Scotch Pond and the Britannia Shipyard, both owned by the City of Richmond.

Paramount Pond was originally a reservoir with a narrow entrance at the west end beside the Colonial Cannery. In 1979 the Small Craft Harbours Branch dredged the land between the river's edge and the south side of the pond to increase its capacity to approximately 400 boats, including those moored along the edges of the pond.

Fewer fishing days and stronger synthetic nets reduced damages to nets substantially. Most net wharves and floats disappeared from the Steveston waterfront. The few remaining net wharves were paved with asphalt and provided with racks of galvanized iron piping. Scotch Pond, which was operated by a co-operative of local independent fishermen, became the only camp where fishermen were still assigned net floats for boat moorage and net repairs. The racks of these floats were made of poles and lumber.

Fishermen

Salmon fishermen relied on higher fish prices to off-set increased operating costs. A steady flow of farmed salmon flooded the market and forced prices down for wild salmon. Older fishermen, and those anxious to leave the fishery sold their licenses to the remaining fishermen or to the government license buy-back programme.

The Japanese fishermen who returned to Steveston after the Second World War began to retire in the 1970s, and all had retired by the 1990s. By 1997 only about fifty descendants of the returnees continued to fish out of Steveston. When Japanese-Canadians gained the right to vote in 1949, they also gained access to all professions, and most descendants of returnees chose to work in the trades, professions, civil service and businesses.

The net wharf at Paramount Pond with asphalt paving and galvanized iron pipe racks. (1995)(MY)

Many boats were sold to Vietnamese fishermen in the 1980s. In 1984 Pham Thom bought the ***SANTA BARBARA*** and started fishing out of Steveston. Two months later, Van Moc Le purchased the ***OCEAN RAINBOW***. There were five Vietnamese salmon fishermen in 1985 and 120 by 1988. Pham Thom was elected chairman of the Vietnamese Fishermen's Association in May 1988.

Fishermen's Fish Market

There were few outlets for species other than salmon and halibut in the early 1970s. Furthermore, when fishermen sold their catches to companies, they received only a fraction of the final product price. To maximize profits, a few fishermen began to market their catches directly to consumers. In the early 1970s Andrew Kromedas started selling bottomfish directly to the public from his ***DEBBIE MAC***. He sold from the public wharf at the end of Second Avenue on an irregular basis.

About the same time Bobby Nishi and his wife started selling beam trawl caught shrimp from their home. About 1974 they started selling from his ***ENSENADA*** at the Second Avenue public dock. They put up signs in Richmond, Vancouver and Surrey advertising fresh shrimp for sale on Sundays in Steveston.

Also about the same time, Frank Ross and Bill Thompson started selling pot-caught prawns from the dock off the ***KARMSUND***. They cooked up a pot of prawns which they took to radio station CKWX. They parleyed the Sunday morning disc jockey into giving three announcements about the sale of prawns at Steveston in exchange for the pot of cooked prawns. They traded cooked prawns for ads for three weeks, and then started paying for the ads.

Phil Geschke (right) of the crabber ***BEV ANNE*** *with Tony Capadouca. Phil regularly sold dungeness crab at the weekend sales, and Tony sold bottomfish for many years from the* ***SILVER BEAR****. (1997)(MY)*

A little later Tony Capadouca began to sell bottomfish off his truck parked at the foot of Second Avenue, but was soon selling off the ***SILVER BEAR***.

These uncoordinated fish sales drew large crowds to the docks, and line-ups to purchase shrimp and fish. Good sales prompted more fishermen to sell greater volumes and other varieties of fish such as crabs, live rock cod, tuna and salmon at the dock. More people were attracted to the Sunday sales, and fishermen started selling on Saturday as well.

The weekend fish market was moved to the outermost finger of the new public wharf at the foot of Third Avenue in the late 1970s, and to the dedicated fish sales wharf off Steveston Landing in 1988. The fish sales became a regular event on the Steveston waterfront on Fridays, Saturdays and Sundays. This popular fishermen's market became a major magnet for local residents and tourists by offering the freshest seafood at the lowest prices in the lower mainland.

New Fisheries, New Hope.

In 1996 twenty-six fish processing companies in Richmond were licensed by the Department of Fisheries and Oceans. After BC Packers closed, Ocean Fisheries was the only one in Richmond operating a salmon canning line. The increase in the number of processors was largely due to the relatively new groundfish fishery. By 1996 the value of the thirty species of groundfish landed in British Columbia was $101,100,000, exceeding $96,305,000 for salmon, $71,300,000 for herring and $6,576,000 for tuna, mackerel and other species. The groundfish fishery had become the largest fishery on the west coast.

Unlike the salmon fishery, which varied widely during a four-year cycle, the groundfish fishery was stable and sustainable, because of a relatively low total allowable catch. While salmon was a seasonal fishery, the groundfish fishery operated year round. Furthermore, the groundfish quota system was designed to encourage unform harvesting along the coast. In 1997 the federal Minister of Fisheries,

Nguyen Van Ut and Hien selling pink and sidestripe shrimp on the ***MANBA A****. The Vietnamese immigrants arrived in the 1980s and became prominent in the salmon, shrimp and crab fisheries. (1997) (MY)*

Fishermen selling their catch from their boats on Steveston Landing wharf. (1997)(MY)

David Anderson, set up the Groundfish Development Authority, to allocate twenty percent of the quota to provide stable market and employment conditions and aid regional development of the fishery in coastal communities.

By 1998 the number of groundfish trawlers using Steveston as their homeport had increased substantially. The groundfish industry needed an adequate deepwater port and off-loading facility that would give independent fishermen direct access to markets. Twelve of these 80 to 150 foot long Canadian vessels were offloading 19 million pounds of groundfish at Bellingham.

In 1998 the Deepsea Trawlers Association requested that the Brunswick-Imperial Cannery site be made available for an offloading facility, market and possible European/Asian style auction capable of offloading an initial capacity of 34 million pounds of groundfish. Of all Canadian sites only Steveston Harbour offered a channel deep enough and broad enough for larger vessels, located near the Strait of Juan de Fuca access to the offshore fishing grounds. This proposal would also provide a major boost to tourism, stability for other segments of the fishing fleet, and the opportunity for many small businesses to supply value-added products to the growing local market catering to the large number of new Asian immigrants.

The Years of Transformation

Chapter

9

1998 - 2005

Townsite and Waterfront

The change from fishing industrial use to residential use was rapid. After 14 months of public information meetings, surveys and advisory committee discussions, BC Packers applied to Richmond Council in October 1997 to develop up to 750 housing units on its 41.4 acres. The proposal included a 3.5 acre waterfront maritime mixed use area with up to 50,000 sq. ft. retail space, 55,000 sq. ft. office space and 44,000 sq. ft industrial space east of Number One Road. Council required the donation of 7.0 acres of waterfront parkland, including the dyke and Phoenix Pond. By June 1998 Council had reduced the park to 3.86 acres, allowing two apartment buildings on the waterfront, partly in exchange for 25,000 sq. ft. library space. Council considered buying more parkland east of Phoenix Pond, but decided $7,700,000 for 3.37 acres was too expensive.

In March 1999 BC Packers sold all its BC processing plants and fishing fleet to CanFisCo, owned by Jimmy Pattison, but retained its BC farm fish operations. In November 1999 the company opened a waterfront trail from Number One Road to Westwater Drive. This "waterfront park" would eventually include public piers, heritage signs and displays of small boats and cannery equipment.

Plans to preserve and reuse the heritage buildings were presented. BC Fishermen's Co-op, led by Chris Day of the Deep Sea Trawlers' Association, proposed an auction center and fish market on the Brunswick/Imperial cannery site. Instead, the Steveston Harbour Authority leased 8,000 square feet of the Paramount Cannery building to Steveston Seafood Auction Incorporated. At the first auction sale on May 21, 1999, 10,000 pounds of fish was sold to commercial buyers. The Steveston Fisheries Alliance, led by Dave Bell, and later Richard Gray and Doug Day, proposed a fish offloading and storage facility at the Cold Storage Building and an auction/fish market at the Brunswick/Imperial site. The Phoenix Cannery Preservation Society under Barry Roughton and Gordon Kibble studied restoring the Phoenix Cannery for a maritime museum and estuarium.

These heritage buildings were on BC Government owned waterlots leased by BC Packers. The BC Packers rezoning had approved a marina and seafood auction on this site. The NDP government postponed a decision on leasing the land until after the BC Provincial election in May 2001, when the

Waterfront view of Imperial Cannery before demolition. (2001)(HS)

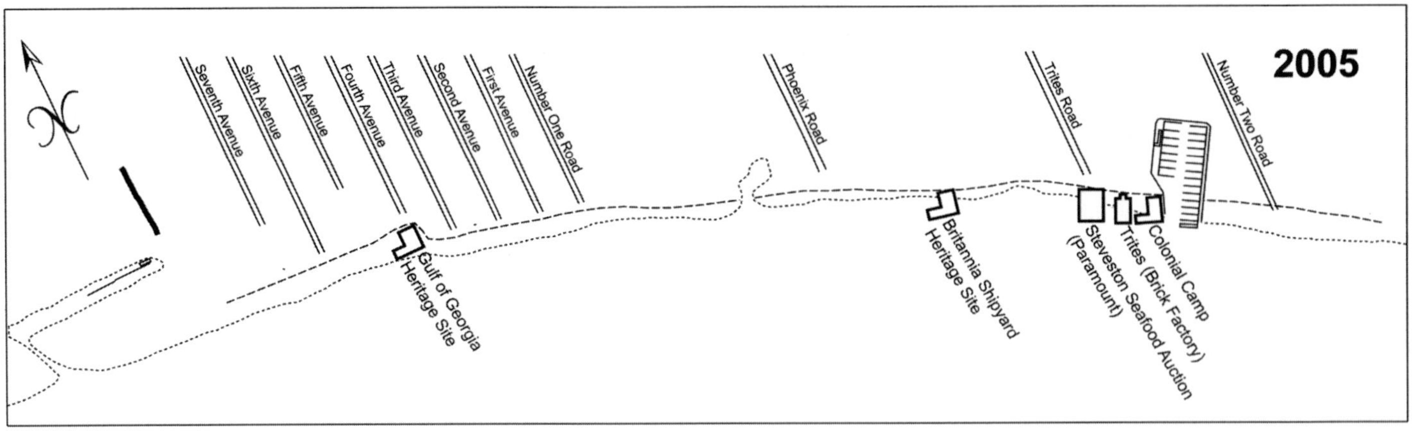

Map of the Steveston waterfront showing location of canneries in 2005. (clear buildings - non-operating)

Liberals led by Gordon Campbell became the government. On May 28, 2001, Richmond Council narrowly approved BC Packers' plans for redevelopment with a final 5/4 vote, opposed by Councillors Linda Barnes, Malcolm Brodie, Harold Steves, and Mayor Greg Halsey-Brandt.

On July 18, 2001, Stan Hagan, the Minister of Sustainable Resources in the new government, gave Richmond Council thirty days to seek viable proposals to redevelop the Brunswick/Imperial Cannery site. Hagan granted Council's request to keep the docks and piers for the planned Tall Ships Event in 2002. On August 8, 2001, Fraser River Port Authority gave BC Packers permission to demolish the cannery buildings and wharves, the two finger piers and 650 feet of dolphins for moorage. The Brunswick/Imperial buildings were bulldozed on August 14, salvageable wood removed, and the wharves and docks destroyed. Only the Phoenix Cannery gillnet loft, built after 1943, remained.

Two months later the Onni Group of Companies purchased the BC Packers property to build 505 low-rise apartment units, 175 townhouses and 69 single-family homes. Construction proceeded rapidly, and by December 2002, 58 single-family homes were advertised for sale. Then 91 condominium apartment units in Copper Sky became available in March 2003, 53 heritage style three level townhouses were offered in September 2003, and 137 more low-rise condominium apartments were on the market in November 2003. Onni got 21 Georgie Awards for Copper Sky at Imperial Landing, including awards for Best Landscape Design, Best Marketing Campaign, and Best Residential Development.

In April 2002 the Steveston Independent School Society, under former Richmond School Principal Roy Akune, purchased the 25,000 square foot BC Packers office building, the only building remaining of the Imperial Cannery Complex, for a private school for 400 students. The Society decided to retain its original facilities, and sold the property

Imperial Cannery being demolished. (2001)(HS)

Waterfront walkway beside newly constructed townhouses and monument to Japanese Canadian fishermen. (2005)(MY)

early in 2005.

In September 2003 Onni presented to Richmond Council a revised plan for 120,000 square feet residential and 70,000 square feet commercial on the 3.5 acres for maritime mixed use. On the 11 acres of land and water-lots outside the dyke now owned or controlled by the City of Richmond, City Staff recommended adding a waterfront restaurant to the seafood auction wharf, and marina previously approved during the BC Packers rezoning.

Garry Point Park

Garry Point Park is named for Nicholas Garry, deputy governor of the Hudson Bay Company from 1822 to 1835. However, it was originally a summer fishing camp for the Musqueam Native Indians, and now honours the fortitude and endurance of all Steveston fishermen.

Kuno Gardens was first established in 1988 to commemorate the 100th anniversary of the arrival of fisherman Gihei Kuno from Wakayama, Japan. This traditional Japanese garden, built by the BC Wakayama Kenjin-Kai, features black pines, Akibono cherry trees and shrubs around a stone bridge and large flat stepping stones. It symbolizes the deep roots Japanese Canadians have made in the Steveston community.

The Fishermen's Memorial Committee unveiled the aluminum fish net mending needle (see photo on page 135) on May 4, 1996, as a memorial to 147 Steveston-based fishermen who lost their lives at sea. The names of these fishermen and their boats are engraved on the carved stonewalls around the needle.

Twenty-five commercial fishermen in the Scotch Pond Heritage Co-operative volunteered to preserve heritage at Scotch Pond, near the site of the former Scottish Canadian Cannery and Atagi Boat Works. They reconstructed cedar docks and five hundred feet of wooden floats to moor fifty boats. Visitors to Garry Point can watch fishermen tending their boats and mending their nets.

Kuno Garden in Garry Point Park. (2005)(MY)

Cannery row: from the left, newly constructed townhouses, frame structure commemorating location of Imperial Cannery, Phoenix gillnet loft and Paramount Cannery. (2005)(MY)

Fraser River Fishing 1997 to 2004

In 1998 the federal government reduced annual license fees from $1,390 to $710 for large gillnetters and from $5,750 to $3,880 for seiners because the landed value of fish catches had dropped 34% between 1994 and 1997. Federal fisheries minister David Anderson, whose great grandfather Jacob Hunter Todd had owned canneries from Steveston to Prince Rupert up to the 1950s, closed coho sports fisheries and required commercial fishermen to release coho caught during sockeye fishing.

A Canadian/U.S. agreement signed in July 1998 reduced American fishermen's coho catch by 22% (7,000 fish) in return for BC fishermen catching 50% less chinook (7,000 fish) bound for Puget Sound. This agreement also raised the American fishermen's share of Fraser River Sockeye from 12.5% to 24.9%.

After temperatures in the Fraser River hit 21 degrees C in early August, the highest recorded level in 87 years, all sports and commercial sockeye fisheries were closed except for one 24 hour opening on August 12, where BC fishermen caught 1,500,000 and Washington fishermen caught 430,000. At the end of 1998 the federal government bought back 42 seine licenses (average $420,152), 20 gillnet licenses (average $77,880) and 33 troll licenses (average $77,532). After the buyback the BC fishing fleet owned 442 seine licenses, 1,805 gillnet licenses and 956 troll licenses.

In 1999 over 8,000,000 sockeye were expected in the Fraser River run, but only 1,300,000 arrived. Experts blamed warm water, low nutrient levels, predators like mackerel and tuna, and high water levels after record snowpacks. Aboriginal fishermen caught 275,900 salmon for food, but there was no commercial fishery at all. Fishermen began to consider buying other fishing licenses, but the prices were very high - $400,000 to catch 20,000 pounds of halibut, $100,000 to catch 160 tons of sardines, or $400,000 to license a fifty foot boat to catch prawns.

Bottomfish trawlers at moorage at the foot of Seventh Avenue. (2005) (MY)

To raise awareness of the fishermen's plight, Ucluelet fisherman Dan Edwards and his daughter Danielle staged a hunger strike outside Steveston's Gulf of Georgia Cannery, living on water, carrot and lemon juice and maple syrup from October 1 to 12, and from October 26 to December 10, when Edwards finally got a meeting with new federal fisheries minister Herb Dhaliwal.

In 2000 commercial fishermen caught 130,000 sockeye salmon in one 24 hour opening for gillnetters and one 24 hour opening for trollers.

In 2001 commercial seineboats harvested 256,000 sockeyes in two openings on the Fraser River, while the gillnet fleet sat tied to the dock for the whole season. Aboriginal fishermen took 397,000 sockeye in "pilot sales" openings, the controversial Native commercial fisheries initiated in 1992 for the Musqueam, Tsawwassen, Burrard and Stolo bands. Between 1996 and 2001 the Fraser River fishing fleet had shrunk dramatically from 1,250 gillnet boats to 407.

In 2002 the total commercial sockeye catch was 2,100,000 fish in 31 hours of openings spread over four days, while sports fishermen took 50,000 fish, Aboriginal fishermen took 1,000,000 and Americans took 440,000.

Other fisheries began to look very inviting. In 2003 the greatest pink salmon run in 40 years resulted in a catch of 7,800,000 but the price to fishermen dropped to ten cents a pound, barely covering operating costs. The 15,400 tonnes of pink salmon caught in BC in 2003 had a landed value of $4,400,000, whereas the relatively new BC groundfish harvest of 126,100 tonnes had a landed value of $135,000,000. The Groundfish Development Authority had been set up in 1996 to allocate quotas and retain processing in coastal communities. Twelve deep sea trawlers were operating out of Steveston, landing their groundfish catch at the Paramount site for trucking, and other sites for processing.

Steveston fishermen also acquired eight out of the 25 new commercial licenses in an expanded sardine fishery, pioneered by Steveston fisherman Byron Wright. Customers in Spain, Portugal and France were paying $1,500 US a tonne for food-grade sardines.

The Native "pilot sales" program was discontinued in 2003 when Judge William Kitchen stayed charges against 140 fishermen who had dropped nets illegally in 1998 to protest the race-based fishery. The judge ruled that the program was "poorly designed and ineffectual", "grossly unfair", "government sponsored racial discrimination". When the BC Supreme Court overturned this provincial court ruling on July 12, 2004, Steveston and Ladner fishermen flew Canadian flags upside

Pleasure crafts moored with fishing boats in Paramount Pond. (2005)(MY)

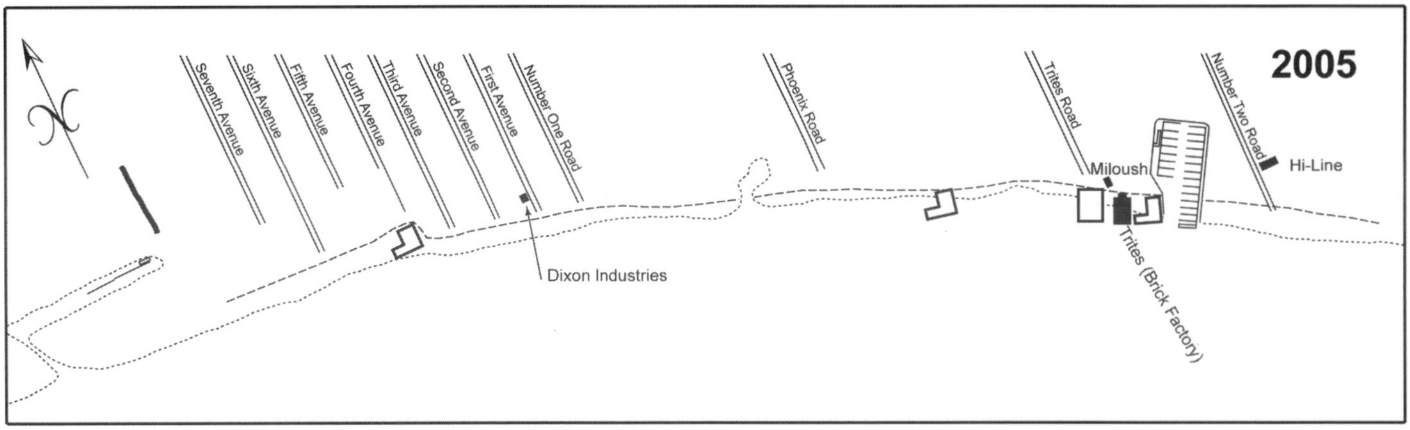

Map of the Steveston waterfront showing locations of boat works in 2005.

down on their boats, an international signal of distress, to protest the Aboriginal only commercial fishery by Musqueam and Tsawwassen Natives on July 29.

There were only three Fraser River openings totalling 39 hours for commercial gillnetters in 2004, when 371 vessels caught 219,000 sockeye salmon. The total Fraser River sockeye catch reported in 2004 was 1,058,600 by BC commercial fishermen, 190,900 by American commercial fishermen, 256,200 by Coastal Aboriginal fishermen, 199,100 by Lower Fraser River Aboriginal fishermen, and 73,700 by test fisheries. Scientists at the Mission hydro-acoustic station estimated that 2,604,600 sockeye salmon passed Mission, but only 250,000 sockeye salmon reached the spawning grounds. Aboriginal fishermen reported catching 427,500 sockeyes above Mission, and 52,200 were caught by sports fishermen.

The Department of Fisheries and Oceans appointed the 2004 Pacific South Coast Salmon Harvest Review Committee to investigate why 1,874,700 fish were missing. Was this disappearance due to habitat deterioration from cities, forestry, agriculture, increased erosion, flooding of watersheds, loss of estuaries, and warmer temperatures? Or was it from unreported catches above Mission?

The committee concluded after several hearings that the major factor was unauthorized aboriginal fishing and lack of federal enforcement and management. While most Native fishermen were complying, newspapers reported that Cheam Band members near Chilliwack openly defied government-ordered closures, and pepper sprayed fisheries officers trying to inspect the Cheam fish-landing sites.

Officials estimated that 12,600,000 sockeye salmon and 16,300,000 pink salmon would return to the Fraser in 2005, a high cycle year for both species.

Boat Works and Fishing Boats

With little prospects for increased fishing time, commercial fishermen continued fishing their old boats. For the first time since the inception of the Fraser River salmon canning industry in 1870, no new gillnetters were added to the fishery. Of the boat works from the previous period, only Hi-Line, Trites and Miloush remained. A recent addition was Dixon Industries in the old Thompson Bros. premises on First Avenue.

Moorage space along the Steveston waterfront became available as increasing numbers of fishermen left the Fraser River fishery. The Phoenix Pond was abandoned for mooring boats because of silting, but remains as part of the foreshore trail. Pleasure boats are increasingly occupying the moorages vacated by fishing boats in Paramount Pond.

Salmon Farming in B.C.

By 1999 Canada was the world's fourth largest producer of farmed salmon, behind only Norway, Chile and the United Kingdom. By 2001 the 107 fish farms in BC, owned by twelve companies, produced more than 70% of Canada's farmed fish harvest, providing an estimated 4,140 direct and indirect jobs to coastal communities.

The 1995 provincial moratorium on fish farm expansion was still in place. More than 345,000 Atlantic salmon had escaped from open net cages on BC fish farms during the 1990s. Environmental groups like the David Suzuki foundation warned that the escaped fish were competing for food and space, disrupting migration, interfering with spawning, digging up eggs and escalating sea lice populations. A report released in April 2001 confirmed that most BC salmon farms were not properly storing and disposing of fish blood waste, sewage, diesel fuels, acids, disinfectants, pesticides and drugs. In September 2001 the Leggatt Inquiry recommended removal of all net cages on salmon farms and no further expansion of fish farming.

In 2000 BC produced 49,000 tonnes of farmed salmon with a landed value of $282,000,000 and a wholesale value of $320,000,000. In comparison, commercial fishermen harvested 18,800 tonnes of wild salmon with a landed value of $50,000,000 and a wholesale value of $154,000,000.

Production rose to 68,000 tonnes of farmed salmon with a wholesale value of only $323,000,000 in 2001, and 84,200 tonnes of farmed salmon with a wholesale value of $359,000,000 in 2002, compared to $199,000,000 for wild salmon, $238,500,000 for groundfish and $129,500,000 for herring. By 2003 the wholesale value of farmed salmon dropped to $308,000,000 for 73,000 tonnes because of disease (Stolt Sea Farms lost a million juvenile fish at one farm), and the dramatic decrease of BC exports to United States when overproduction in Chile caused a major drop in prices and demand.

In July 2003 the Canadian Centre for Policy Alternatives released a report titled "Fishy Business: the Economics of Salmon Farming in BC." They estimated salmon farms generated only 1,900 jobs, compared to 5,400 jobs by commercial fisheries, 8,900 jobs by sports fisheries, and 3,900 jobs in seafood processing.

In addition, consumers were becoming increasingly concerned about the high level of PCBs (poly chlorinated biphenyls), fat and antibiotics in farmed salmon. In January 2004 a study by the "Environmental Protection Agency" released a report in Science magazine recommending a maximum of one meal of farmed salmon per person per month, and stating the healthiest fish to eat were wild pink salmon and wild chum salmon. Farmed fish contain twice as much fat as wild fish because their diet is high in fish oil from forage fish. They have 11 times as much PCBs, and require antibiotics, drugs and pesticides because they are so densely stocked in net cages (16 kg. of fish per cubic metre) and prone to stress, injury and disease.

In 2004 the two largest BC farmed salmon producers merged to trim costs. Sales of farmed salmon had been plummeting due to oversupply, competition from Chile, the rising Canadian dollar and environmental and health concerns. This also affected the prices for wild salmon.

The third largest producer, George Weston Limited, a multinational grocery giant that owns Loblaws and Great Canadian

*Steveston Seabreeze Adventures office and the **TRIPLE 8 II** on the government wharf at the foot of Number One Road. (2005)(MY)*

Superstore, had bought out BC Packers in 1969. The company closed the last major fish cannery in Steveston in 1992, and shut down the fresh fish processing in the Steveston Imperial plant in 1996, planning to concentrate on farmed salmon operations on its 13 BC fish farms employing 150 people. In February 2005, claiming a $25,000,000 annual loss, the company listed for sale all its Heritage Salmon fish farming operations in British Columbia, New Brunswick and Maine, valued at $250,000,000.

Whale Watching Tour Companies

Cedric Towers opened the Vancouver Whale Watch office on Second Avenue and started taking passengers out on whale watching tours in 1998. The company operates three whale watching boats. The ***EXPLORATHOR*** and ***EXPLORATHOR EXPRESS*** are semi-enclosed Zodiac boats, each capable of carrying 40 passengers, and the ***LIGHTSHIP I*** is an open Zodiac boat, with capacity for 12 passengers. The company conducts whale watching tours from April through October, primarily in the southern Gulf of Georgia and eastern Juan de Fuca. The company also conducts a nature and historical tour of Steveston Cannery Row with the ***RIVER QUEEN***. Vancouver Whale Watch boats moor on the easternmost boat float at Steveston Landing.

Bobby Morimoto, Lloyd Nakade and Rick Thompson formed Steveston Seabreeze Adventures in 1999 and started whale and sea lion watching tours and fishing charters. The Seabreeze Adventures office is located on the Public Wharf at the foot of Number One Road. The company operates three super punts and a gillnetter. The ***TRIPLE 8 II*** is licensed to carry 23 passengers for whale/sea lion watching, while the ***TRIPLE 8*** and ***CRAZY-LEGS*** carry 12 passengers for whale/sea lion watching and fishing charters. The ***HI-VOLTAGE*** carries 7 passengers on fishing charters

Richmond Tall Ships Festival

On July 11th, 2002, 10,000 people at Garry Point Park welcomed the ***NIPPON MARU*** as she sailed to the Number Three Road pier. A few days later 5,000 spectators watched the crew demonstrate how to set up the sails and unfurl them. This 360-foot four-masted barque was built in 1984 in Japan for students of mercantile marine schools. Her crew was especially welcome because many fishermen had emigrated from the Wakayama area in Japan to Steveston around 1900.

In the summer of 2002 Richmond was the only Canadian city to host the Tall Ships Challenge Series, an event promoted by the American Sail Training Association (ASTA) based in Rhode Island. Richmond City Council arranged and paid for almost all the preparation and operation of this festival from August 8th

NIPPON MARU *moored to the fishing wharf at the foot of Number 3 Road. (2002)(HS)*

to 12th. The City also spent $100,000 to extend the waterfront walkway from the Third Avenue pier to Steveston Landing, and $400,000 to upgrade the Number Three Road pier and add a float large enough for 350-foot ships, both long-lasting community improvements. The federal government contributed approximately $1,000,000 towards dredging the Steveston Harbour deep enough for the sailing ships, and the BC Lotteries Corporation donated $25,000 to build the Lotto 6/49 20th Anniversary community stage at the foot of Third Avenue. Audiences also saw free performances at the YVR Sea to Sky stage in Garry Point Park. Over 2,100 volunteers helped co-ordinate equipment and organize visitors.

Other attractions were the Salmon Bake put on by Richmond Rod and Gun Club, the Pancake breakfast by the Steveston Lions Club, the Model Boat Competition at Richmond City Hall, the Heat Stroke youth music festival at Steveston Park, and the Captain's Ball hosted by the Rotary Club at Vancouver Airport Conference resort, but the real draw was the ships.

On Thursday, August 8th, over 135,000 people crowded onto Garry Point to witness the arrival of twenty-four sailing ships, causing the biggest traffic jam in Richmond's history, packed parking lots, a need for fifty additional buses, and two-hour line-ups to view the boats. These ships ranged from the ***MUNIN***, a 40-foot half-size Viking ship replica built in Burnaby by the Scandinavian Culture Society, to the ***EUROPA***, a 180-foot three-masted barque built in 1911 in the Netherlands.

The Snowbirds, nine Canadian CT 114 tutor jets from the Canadian Forces, flew over the eager watchers before the ships appeared, led by the ***MAPLE LEAF***, a 90-foot Canadian schooner. The ***ZODIAC***, a 160-foot two-masted gaff-rigged schooner, anchored at the Number Three Road pier. The ***NINA***, a 92-foot caravel replica built in the Virgin Islands to commemorate the 500th anniversary of Christopher Columbus' discovery of America, was moored near Britannia Shipyard. The others were spread along the docks between Number One Road and Seventh Avenue.

On Sunday, August 11th, the ***LADY WASHINGTON***, a 112-foot brigantine, and

Spectators at Garry Point welcoming the ***EUROPA*** *entering Steveston Harbour. (2002)(HS)*

The ***NINA*** *moored at the Britannia Shipyard Historical Site, with townhouses in the background. (2002)(HS)*

the ***HAWAIIAN CHIEFTAIN***, a 103-foot square top-sail ketch, entertained spectators with a mock battle off Garry Point, exchanging cannon fire and using long boats.

A single ticket enabled a visitor to tour all the ships. Thirty thousand of these tickets were sold for $10 each before the ships arrived. Prestigious Admiral's Club VIP tickets for $50 each allowed the holder to avoid line-ups and get into the Admiral's Club on the Seventh Avenue pier. Over 400,000 visitors in five days generated an estimated economic spin-off to local businesses of $11,300,000. On August 12th the ships left Richmond for Seattle and San Francisco, 650 nautical miles away.

Horizon Multimedia released 500 copies of a video filmed by Jennifer and Jan Vozenilek recording the Tall Ships in Steveston. John Horton, an internationally-renowned Steveston artist, sold copies of his specially-commissioned painting entitled "Days of Glory" for $400 each, donating half of the proceeds to support the Tall Ships Festival.

ASTA presented the City of Richmond with the 2002 Port City of the Year award. However, Richmond Council decided not to repeat the event in 2005, after Parks and Recreation staff reported a sizeable loss for the Tall Ships event, due to low corporate sponsorship, inadequate government grants, and unexpected expenses on landside venues. Council offered to contribute $350,000 of staff time to a 2005 event, but would not grant the loan for $150,000 requested for 2005 by the Richmond Tall Ships 2002 Coordinating Committee, chaired by Janice Podmore. The Tall Ships event went to Vancouver in 2005.

On July 13th, 2004, the Japanese ship ***KAIWO MARU***, a 361-foot four-masted barque, docked at the Number Three Road pier for a four day visit to mark the City's 125th anniversary. The name of this sister ship of the ***NIPPON MARU*** means "King of the Sea".

On July 26th, 2004, the ***CONCORDIA***, a 188-foot three-masted barkentine with 10,000 square feet of sail, berthed at Britannia Shipyard. This ship gives Grade 11 and 12 students in Canada and United States a chance to spend an entire academic year sailing around the world. The crew offered day-long excursions for $50 per passenger with instruction in "seamanship, sail manoeuvres, knot tying and safety" between July 30 and August 13. Then the ship made headlines across Canada when she ran aground on a sandbar at low tide on her first trip, and fifty passengers had to be rescued by a Coast Guard hovercraft. Fortunately no lasting damage resulted, and on August 4th the excursions continued as planned.

*The **MUNIN** moored at the Gulf of Georgia Historical Site. (2002)(HS)*

Epilogue

The Steveston waterfront has changed tremendously since 1889 when William Herbert Steves first promoted his scheme to develop the principal port on the Fraser River. The first Steveston cannery was built in 1882 and the last in 1957. Between 1889 and 1905 twenty-one more canneries were built along a one and a half mile stretch of river frontage, the largest cannery row with the highest density of salmon canneries in the world. Two of these canneries never operated. The Dumfries Cannery was a "dummy", built only to qualify for the twenty fishing licenses allotted to each cannery in the early 1890s. The original Star Cannery was destroyed by fire, but was rebuilt in time for the 1895 fishing season. Many canneries operated for fewer than ten years. Fifteen canneries operated in 1899, 1900 and 1901. The Imperial Cannery stopped canning salmon in 1992 after operating for 100 years. Only two other canneries operated for more than fifty years, the Phoenix and the Great West.

The Fraser River gillnetter evolved through the years from a small wooden skiff to a large aluminium, twin-engine vessel. The original craft developed for the Fraser River gillnet fishery was a flat-bottomed skiff propelled by two men with oars and an auxiliary sail. This skiff cost $26. The roundbottomed Columbia River type boat was introduced in the late 1880s and the gasoline engine-powered gillnet boat became the standard in the 1910s. The gillnet drum was invented and gained wide acceptance in the late 1930s. Fibreglass reinforced plastic (FRP) became a popular building material for small vessels in the 1970s, superseded by aluminium in the 1980s. In the 1990s the latest variant for gillnetting salmon and herring was the super punt, an aluminium planing hull vessel powered with twin diesel engines coupled with water jet propulsion engines, and capable of attaining speeds of 35 mph. The super punt cost approximately $150,000.

The early labour-intensive salmon canning industry required large numbers of workers on the canning lines and fishermen to crew the small catcher boats. Salmon canning villages became centres of racial diversity, as ethnic groups sought employment. They were housed in segregated buildings supplied by the canneries. From the beginning Caucasian men monopolized the managerial, technical and supervisory tasks. Steveston canneries in the 1880s were manned primarily by Native women and Chinese men, while Native men fished from canoes and Fraser River skiffs. Caucasian and Japanese fishermen gained prominence in the 1890s. With the Smith butchering machine and increasing mechanization of the canning process in the 1900s, fewer Chinese workers were contracted. Japanese women replaced Native women on the sliming and canning lines in the 1910s. The Japanese dominated Steveston from the 1890s to 1942, when all Japanese-Canadian families were evacuated en masse to internment camps in the British Columbia interior and to other provinces.

Racial antagonism on the canning lines was common, but rarely erupted into communal conflicts, since each ethnic group had designated tasks and there was little competition between groups. However, on the

Remains of wood dyke along the Britannia Shipyard site. The wood dyke and boardwalk were originally made along the Steveston townsite and eventually extended along the entire waterfront. (1997) (MY)

fishing grounds, competition was rife among Native, Caucasian and Japanese fishermen. During strikes and negotiations of fish prices, cannery owners fuelled the strife between groups by threatening the Japanese with eviction. In the most violent Steveston strike of 1900 the provincial government fearful of rioting, declared martial law to maintain law and order.

Discrimination against the Japanese fostered their segregation into a tight, self-contained community in Steveston. In 1897 they formed the Japanese Fishermen's Association to champion better prices and working conditions. When the Richmond School Board passed a law entitling only children of property owners to attend public schools, the Japanese built their own school to educate their children. Later they managed to integrate their children into the public school system by contributing to the construction of two new school buildings. Japanese parents wanted their children to speak English before entering public school. The United Church and the Japanese Women's Association (Fujinkai) and the Catholic Sisters of Atonement started kindergarten classes to teach English to Japanese children, fifty years before kindergartens became common.

Frequent outbreaks of typhoid fever also plagued Steveston. With no clean supply of potable water, Steveston inhabitants often used the polluted river water for drinking, cooking and washing. The Japanese were especially afflicted, because of crowded living conditions on shore and inadequate facilities for boiling water on their boats. The Japanese Methodist Mission, built in 1895 on the Phoenix Cannery premises to care for the sick, was so successful that the Fishermen's Benevolent Society built a larger hospital for the Japanese community. For a nominal annual fee, subscribers were provided with consultations, medication and hospital beds. Thus the Japanese community in Steveston had Medicare sixty years before the general Canadian public.

The design of net guards for wooden gillnetters had not changed in sixty years. (1971)(MY)

Racial discrimination of visible minorities was sanctioned by law in Canada until 1949, when the Natives, East Indians, Chinese and Japanese finally got the right to vote. During the first decades of this century, Japan's military excursions into Korea and China made Japanese immigrants the ideal scapegoats for ambitious politicians and ordinary citizens with real or imagined grievances. The surprise attack on Pearl Harbour by the Japanese Imperial Navy in December 1941 brought discrimination against the Japanese to a head. Fearing fifth column activities by local Japanese in a possible invasion of the British Columbia coast, the public demanded their expulsion from the coast. Martial law was imposed again, giving Steveston the dubious distinction of being called under martial law on two separate occasions, both centred on imagined threats by the Japanese.

The labours of Native, Chinese and Japanese races sustained the salmon canning industry in Steveston for its first fifty years. However, very few artifacts remained in Steveston in 1997 to attest to the past importance of these visible minorities. A restored boat works and an abandoned cannery house were all that remained of the Japanese past. Only a dilapidated net shed converted from an Indian longhouse testified to the Native presence in the village. A Chinese bunk house, shipped down from Knight Inlet, was the only testimonial to the Chinese past.

Steveston survived many disasters. The most severe natural disaster was the flood of 1905, which affected much of the southwestern corner of Lulu Island, but did relatively little damage because of the low permanent population. Several fires consumed the Steveston waterfront, destroying ten of the canneries and much of the town. The Star, Phoenix and Dumfries were burnt in 1895. Four fires in the 1900s ravaged various sections of the waterfront, including "China town" along Number One Road and another "China town" near the Hong Wo general store. The Burrard Cannery was reportedly burned in 1910. The 1918 fire razed the rebuilt Star, Steveston and Lighthouse Canneries and a large part of the town site. In 1924 another fire destroyed the Richmond and Canadian Pacific Canneries and numerous cannery houses. Fire demolished the Great West Cannery in 1961. The empty Phoenix Cannery was partially consumed by fire in 1997.

For over a hundred years from the 1880s to the 1980s, the economic base of Steveston was fishing. The salmon canning industry expanded rapidly in the late Nineteenth Century when investors believed salmon was an unlimited resource. Canneries were mechanized and amalgamated early in the Twentieth Century to compete successfully with American trap fisheries. In 1913 the Hell's Gate obstruction caused a catastrophic decline in Fraser River salmon runs and further consolidations. Fraser River salmon stocks generally prospered after the International Pacific Salmon Commission rebuilt decimated runs in the 1940s. The cannery closures and consolidations after 1960 were caused by improvements in canning technology, salmon farming, the GATT agreement and new markets for fresh, frozen, smoked and salted fish.

By 1997 there were no operating canneries left on the Steveston waterfront, only abandoned canneries, converted net and gear storage sheds, and heritage buildings. The waterfront remained an exclusive haven for fishing vessels with boat basins, wharves, boat and net floats and storage facilities. However, with the rising value of waterfront properties, its future as an enclave strictly for fishing boats was uncertain.

The economic base of the town shifted to tourism in the 1990s. Two major attractions were its unique waterfront lined with a large variety of fishing vessels, and its colourful weekend fishermen's market. Part of Steveston's multicultural heritage was still alive in the Japanese Buddhist Temple, Martial Arts Centre and the Japanese Community Drop-In Centre. Historic sites like the Britannia Heritage Shipyard and the Gulf of Georgia Cannery presented Steveston's unique industrial history.

After 2000 much of the Steveston Industrial Park at Number Two Road and Moncton Street and all of the B.C. Packers site were re-developed for housing and waterfront condominiums. With the Fraser River fleet idle for much of the year, and only a dozen deepsea trawlers fishing full time, the once proud "Salmon Capital of the World" had become a bedroom community and tourist destination.

Cannery row: from the right, the Colonial net shed, Trites Marine (formerly BC Pressed Brick), the Paramount net shed, the abandoned Pacific Coast Cannery and the Phoenix Cannery. (1995)(MY)

Bibliography

General References

anonymous, *A Dream of Riches: the Japanese Canadians, 1877-1977.* The Japanese Canadian Centennial Project, 1978

Adachi, K., *The Enemy That Never Was: a History of the Japanese Canadians.* McClelland and Stewart Ltd., Toronto, Ontario, 1976

Bannister, M. and M. Clayton, *Steambox, Boardwalks, Belts and Ways: Stories from Britannia.* Britannia Heritage Shipyard Oral History Project, Volume 1, Britannia Heritage Shipyard Society, 1992.

Elliot, Marie, *Mayne Island and the Outer Gulf Islands: a History.* Gulf Islands Press, Box 79, Mayne Island, B.C., 1984.

Dawe, Alan, *Richmond and its Bridges: Fifteen Crossings of the Fraser River.* City of Richmond Archives, Richmond, B.C., 1996.

Gladstone, Percy, *Industrial Disputes in the Commercial Fisheries of B.C.* M.A. thesis, University of B.C., 1959.

Graham, Donald, Keepers of the Light: *A History of British Columbia's Lighthouses and their Keepers*. Harbour Publishing Co. Ltd., Madeira Park, B.C., 1987

Ham, L. *An Archaeological Heritage Resource Overview of Richmond, B.C.* Richmond Museum, Department of Leisure Services, The Corporation of the Township of Richmond, 1987.

Kidd, T., *History of Richmond Municipality.* Wrigley Printing Ltd., Vancouver, B.C., 1927.

Ladner, E.G., *Above the Sand Heads: Firsthand Accounts of Pioneering in the Area Which , in1879, Became the Municipality of Delta, British Columbia.* D.W. Friesen & Sons Ltd., Cloverdale, B.C., 1979.

Lawrence, J.C., *An Historical Account of the Early Salmon Canning Industry in British Columbia, 1870-1900.* B.A. thesis, University of B.C., 1951.

Lyons, C., *Salmon, Our Heritage: The Story of a Province and an Industry.* British Columbia Packers, Vancouver, B.C., 1969.

Marlatt, D., *Steveston Recollected.* Provincial Archives of British Columbia, Victoria, B.C., 1975.

McKervill, H., *The Salmon People: The Story of Canada's West Coast Salmon Fishing Industry.* Gray's Publishing Ltd., Sidney, B.C., 1967.

Meggs, Geoff, *Salmon: The Decline of the British Columbia Fishery.* Douglas and McIntyre, Vancouver, B.C., 1991.

Mitsui, Tadashi, *The Ministry of the United Church of Canada Among Japanese Canadians in British Columbia.* M.A. thesis, Union College of British Columbia, University of B.C., 1964

Newell, Diane, *The Development of the Pacific Salmon Canning Industry: A Grown Man's Game.* McGill-Queens University Press, Montreal, Quebec/Kingston, Ontario, 1989.

O'Bannon, Patrick W., *Waves of Change: Mechanization of the Pacific Coast Canned-Salmon Industry, 1864-1914.* Technology and Culture, Vol. 28, No. 3, 1987.

Reid, D., *The Development of the Fraser River Salmon Canning Industry, 1885 - 1913.* Pacific Region, Department of the Environment, Economics and Sociology Unit, Vancouver, B.C., 1973.

Roos, John F., *Restoring Fraser River Salmon: a History of the International Pacific Salmon Fisheries Commission, 1937-1985.* The Pacific Salmon Commission, Vancouver, B.C., 1991.

Ross, L.J., *Richmond: Child of the Fraser*. Richmond '79 Centennial Society, Richmond, B.C., 1979.
Rounsefell, G.A. and G.B. Kelez, *The Salmon Fisheries of Swiftsure Bank, Puget Sound and the Fraser River.* U.S. Dept. of Commerce, Bureau of Fisheries, Bull. No. 27, 1938.
Sparrow, L., *Work histories of a Coast Salish Couple*. M.A. thesis, University of B.C., 1976.
Stacey, D., *Sockeye and Tinplate: Technological Change in the Fraser River Canning Industry, 1871-1912.* Heritage Record No. 15, British Columbia Provincial Museum, Victoria, B.C., 1982.
Stewart, H., *Indian Fishing: Early Methods on the Northwest Coast.* J.J. Douglas Ltd., Vancouver, B.C., 1977.
Sumida, Regenda, *The Japanese in British Columbia.* M.A. thesis, University of B.C., 1935.
Turner, Robert D., *The Pacific Princesses: an Illustrated History of the Canadian Pacific Railway's Princess Fleet on the Northwest Coast.* Sono Nis Press, Victoria, B.C., 1977.
White, Howard, *They Don't Make Them Anymore: Peck Easthope*, Raincoast Chronicles, No. 5, undated.
Yee, P., *Salt Water City: an Illustrated History of the Chinese in Vancouver.* Douglas & McIntyre, Vancouver, B.C., 1988.

Prologue

anonymous, *"A Cannery Town in Winter"* in Man-to-Man Magazine, January 1911.
Cowen, J. B., *"The Queerest Town in Canada"* in Busy Man's Magazine, March 1910.
Frost, S., *"Steveston's School for Japanese is Busy Place"* in Weekend Magazine, Vancouver Province, November 21, 1936.
Luce, P.W., *"Fishy Business"* in Maclean's Magazine, March 1, 1937.
McEvoy, B., *From the Great Lakes to the Wide West.* William Briggs, Toronto, 1902.
Weston, G., *"Steveston-by-the-Fraser"* in British Columbia Magazine, Vol. 7, No. 8, August 1911.

The Years of Discovery

Doyle, H., *The Quick and the Dead.* manuscript, Doyle Papers , Special Collections, University of B.C., undated.

The Years of Development

Canada B.C. Fisheries Commission Report, Sessional Papers, 1893.
Koyama, Shigeharu, *Nikkei Kanada Imin no Chichi, Homma Tomekichi o no Shogai* Wakayama-ken, Mihama-cho, 1995.
Melvin, George, *The Post Offices of British Columbia.* Wayside Press Ltd., Vernon, B.C., 1972.
THE NEW CANADIAN, Toronto, Ontario, Jun. 7, 1977; Jun. 10, 1977; Jun. 17, 1977; Jun. 21, 1977; Jun. 24, 1977.

The Years of Expansion

anonymous, *Suchibusuton Gyosha Jizen Dantai Sanjugonen Shi.* Suchibusuton Gyosha Jizen Dantai, Steveston, B.C., 1935.
Barry, P.J., *Mackinaw and Collingwood Skiffs*. Yachting LXVIII, Nov., 1940.
Gladstone, Percy, *Native Indians and the Fishing Industry of B.C.* The Canadian Journal of Economics and Political Science, Vol. 19, No. 1, Feb. 1953.
HENDERSON'S British Columbia Gazetteer and Directory. L.G. Henderson, Victoria, B.C., 1898 and 1899.

Large, R.G., *Drums and Scalpel: from Native Healers to Physicians on the North Pacific Coast.*Mitchell Press Ltd., 1968.
WILLIAMS' British Columbia Directory 1891, R.T. Williams, Victoria, B.C., 1891.

The Years of Consolidation and Mechanization

Gilhousen, Philip, *Estimation of Fraser River Escapements from Commercial Harvest Data.* International Pacific Salmon Fisheries Commission, Bull. 27, 1992.
Haig-Brown, Alan, *Fishing for a Living.* Harbour Publishing, Madeira Park, B.C., 1993.
HENDERSON'S British Columbia Gazetteer and Directory. L. G. Henderson, Victoria, B.C., 1903, 1904, 1905 and 1910.
VANCOUVER DAILY PROVINCE, Vancouver, B.C., Oct. 8, 1901; Apr. 5, 1907; Apr. 9, 1907; Oct. 5, 1908.
THE VANCOUVER DAILY SUN, May 15, 1918.

The Years of Uncertainty

anonymous, Annual Reports of the Women's Missionary Society of the United Church, 1924-1940.
Boggis, Steve, *A History of Public Schools in Richmond, 1877 - 1979.* Richmond School Board, 1979.
Kimura, K., unpublished papers, Japanese Canadian Collection, Special Collections, University of B.C.
THE NEW CANADIAN, Toronto, Ontario, Jun. 10, 1977.
VANCOUVER DAILY PROVINCE, Vancouver, British Columbia, May 12, 1924.
THE VANCOUVER SUN, VANCOUVER, B. C., May 12, 1924.
Watada, Terry, Bukkyo Tozen: A History of Jodo Shinshu Buddhism in Canada, 1905-1995, HpF Press and The Toronto Buddhist Church, Toronto, Ont., 1996.
Wild, Paula, *Sointula: Island Utopia.* Harbour Publishing, Madeira Park, B.C., 1995.
WRIGLEY'S British Columbia Directory, Wrigley's Directories Ltd., Vancouver, B. C., 1920 and 1930.

The Years of Upheaval

anonymous, Richmond Berry Growers Association, Japanese-Canadian Collection, Special Collections, University of B. C.
THE BRITISH COLUMBIA AND YUKON DIRECTORY, Sun Directories, Vancouver, B.C., 1941.

The Years of Renewal

anonymous, *Nelson's New Paramount Plant: Speed, Efficiency and Glitter.* Western Fisheries, Aug. 1957.
VANCOUVER DAILY PROVINCE, Vancouver, B.C., Oct. 16, 1961.
THE VANCOUVER SUN, Vancouver, B.C., Apr. 13, 1953

The Years of Decline

anonymous, *Annual Statistical Review of Canadian Fisheries, 1955-1976.* Vol. 9. Marketing Services Division, Fisheries and Marine Service, Environment Canada, Ottawa, 1977.
anonymous, *Building in Wood: the Art of Wooden Boat Building is Alive in Steveston.* Western Fisheries, Mar. 1990.
anonymous, *Summer Launch, **MICKLEY**, a New Boat in the Family Tradition.* Western Fisheries, Aug. 1990.

anonymous, *Fisheries Production Statistics of British Columbia, 1993.* Aquaculture and Commercial Fisheries Branch, Ministry of Agriculture, Fisheries and Food, Province of B.C., 1996.
Keller, Betty C., and Rosella M. Leslie, *Sea-Silver: Inside British Columbia's Salmon Farming Industry.* Horsdal and Schubart Publishers Ltd., Victoria, B.C., 1996.
Meggs, Geoff, *Hello Steveston, Goodbye Vietnam.* THE FISHERMAN, Vancouver, B.C., Nov. 17, 1989.

The Years of Transformation

anonymous, *The 2003 British Columbia Seafood Industry in Review.*Ministry of Agriculture Food and Fisheries, Victoria, B.C., 2004
Cummins, John (MP), and the BC Fisheries Survival Coalition, *2004 Fraser River Escapement Crisis.*2004
THE VANCOUVER SUN, Jan. 9, 2004

Monument in Garry Point Park to Steveston fishermen lost at sea. (2005)(MY)

Index of Steveston People

(by last name only)

(pages includes references in text, photo captions and maps)

Index of Canneries and Companies

(pages include references in text, photo captions and maps)

Canneries

Companies

Appendix Table I. Fraser River sockeye salmon landings by Canada, Canadian Natives and the United States, 1890 - 1995 (source: Pacific Salmon Commission statistics)

Year	Canada	Can. Nat.	U.S.	Year	Canada	Can. Nat.	U.S.	Year	Canada	Can. Nat.	U.S.
1890	2500	250	160	1926	1210	40	470	1962	992	137	759
1891	1800	300	545	1927	860	50	1070	1963	880	190	1314
1892	800	100	400	1928	399	35	630	1964	612	146	508
1893	7000	450	840	1929	846	60	1375	1965	1168	121	1026
1894	3800	200	545	1930	1354	70	3545	1966	2050	154	1337
1895	4200	200	1115	1931	695	45	975	1967	3256	107	2087
1896	3260	60	1180	1932	977	50	855	1968	1322	124	882
1897	12000	400	4465	1933	852	55	1730	1969	2200	159	1575
1898	2200	50	2845	1934	1682	65	3590	1970	2720	151	1350
1899	5200	100	6855	1935	1288	30	615	1971	4045	154	2750
1900	1800	40	2595	1936	2530	60	455	1972	1619	135	1124
1901	12000	400	15195	1937	1673	60	895	1973	2973	164	2560
1902	2850	50	4330	1938	2025	65	1410	1974	4176	222	2460
1903	2200	50	2050	1939	863	40	555	1975	869	253	1556
1904	870	30	1590	1940	1487	45	655	1976	1964	233	1320
1905	11350	400	10170	1941	2690	53	1560	1977	2691	244	1787
1906	2070	50	2040	1942	5783	47	2935	1978	5320	238	1360
1907	690	30	1085	1943	457	27	240	1979	2957	292	1769
1908	870	50	1885	1944	1096	43	435	1980	1604	216	465
1909	7260	370	15490	1945	1263	44	506	1981	4546	460	1293
1910	1690	100	2785	1946	4610	50	3551	1982	6656	430	2867
1911	730	50	1450	1947	544	42	88	1983	4176	379	469
1912	1360	120	2005	1948	898	65	1089	1984	2937	416	1635
1913	10000	300	22035	1949	1335	80	1057	1985	8309	505	2925
1914	2140	120	3555	1950	1250	88	1221	1986	8819	636	2755
1915	1090	30	735	1951	1580	85	1137	1987	3259	573	1923
1916	375	40	920	1952	1461	84	1113	1988	1176	489	679
1917	1880	150	5150	1953	2413	113	2032	1989	12152	696	243
1918	240	20	580	1954	4849	95	4806	1990	12458	1058	2427
1919	470	10	805	1955	1267	66	1007	1991	6282	874	1881
1920	530	10	675	1956	1022	65	907	1992	3528	439	692
1921	485	10	1200	1957	1953	97	1689	1993	13934	1147	2883
1922	580	10	520	1958	9572	83	5257	1994	10035	1191	2068
1923	360	20	505	1959	1945	65	1810	1995	798	873	438
1924	440	40	770	1960	1490	84	1199				
1925	455	60	1375	1961	1948	137	1378				

Apendix Table 2. Gillnet licenses by ethnic groups in the Fraser River, 1877-1934. (source: Rounsefell and Kelez, 1938)

Year	Company	Native	White	Japanese	Other	Total
1877		285				285
1878		449				449
1879		304				304
1880		274				274
1881		396				396
1882		666				666
1883		715	49			764
1884		645	57			702
1885		611	44			655
1886		625	109			734
1887		615	320			935
1888		323	167	10		500
1889		308	167	25		500
1890		308	167	25		500
1891		283	167	50		500
1892		373	240	108		721
1893		558	381	235		1174
1894		549	701	417		1667
1895		539	731	434	30	1734
1896		530	1130	926	60	2646
1897		520	780	928	90	2318
1898		511	690	1321	120	2642
1899		501	710	1361	150	2722
1900	393	555	1076	1659		3683
1901	416	396	909	1805		3526
1902	381	583	781	929		2674
1903	343	477	860	1416		3096
1904	232	446	742	795		2215
1905	339	464	915	1056		2774
1906	200	392	660	494		1746
1907	193	270	494	769		1726
1908	3	175	273	717	195	1363
1909		584	638	1263	243	2728
1910		236	426	766	148	1576
1911		232	411	607	146	1396
1912		217	486	655	72	1430
1913		476	843	1132	109	2560
1914		333	842	1250	231	2656
1915		317	768	1332	199	1616
1916		211	437	1435	157	2240
1917		300	570	1520	237	2627
1918		106	303	1025	149	1583
1919		56	294	874	113	1337
1920		36	275	875	102	1288
1921		68	359	857	153	1437
1922		32	277	871	116	1296
1923		26	304	523	111	964
1924		40	289	523	117	969
1925		36	357	444	132	969
1926		53	429	444	137	1063
1927		58	619	400	172	1249
1928		57	695	400	151	1303
1929		73	830	400	170	1473
1930		60	863	400	200	1523
1931		35	739	400	184	1358
1932		26	840	400	180	1446
1933		25	1026	400	234	1685
1934		31	1105	400	267	1803

Appendix Table 3. Maximum counts of fishing boats on the Fraser River. (source: Pacific Salmon Commission statistics)

Year	Number of Boats
1945	1151
1946	1843
1947	1072
1948	1067
1949	1224
1950	1048
1951	1146
1952	1466
1953	1398
1954	1798
1955	1340
1956	1046
1957	1341
1958	2237
1959	1329
1960	1339
1961	1486
1962	1262
1963	1312
1964	1357
1965	1348
1966	1474
1967	1596
1968	1403
1969	1110
1970	1016
1971	1122
1972	922
1973	1161
1974	1300
1975	977
1976	733
1977	1050
1978	1199
1979	975
1980	607
1981	692
1982	693
1983	665
1984	782
1985	891
1986	920
1987	1060
1988	707
1989	1577
1990	1465
1991	1060
1992	815
1993	1279
1994	1131
1995	1084

About the Authors:

Mitsuo Yesaki was born in the Steveston Japanese Hospital, and is a descendant of three generations of Fraser River fishermen. He fished a "mosquito" skiff from 1952 to 1958. He earned a BSc from the University of British Columbia, and completed courses for a MSc from the Institute of Fisheries. From 1963 to 1966 he was employed by the US Fish and Wildlife Service at the Exploratory Fishing and Gear Research Base in Juneau, Alaska. He worked with the Food and Agriculture Organization of the United Nations from 1967 to 1993, with short breaks in 1970 and 1983. He was assigned to various fisheries projects in the Caribbean, Central America, South America, Middle East, Southeast Asia and South Asia. He has lived in Vancouver since 1993.

Harold and Kathy Steves and their five children moved back to the original family farm in Steveston 100 years after Harold's greatgrandfather Manoah founded it in 1877. They also established a ranch at Savona. Harold was raised on the family farm, worked in his uncle's boat works and at the Phoenix Cannery, fished in the "mosquito fleet", and taught school in Richmond until 1993. He was elected to Richmond City Council in 1969, serving over 30 years. He also championed environmental, farm and fisheries issues as Richmond's provincial MLA from 1972 to 1975. He became Chairperson of the new Groundfish Development Authority in 1998. He was instrumental in bringing the tall ships to Steveston in 2002. Kathy grew up in Nanaimo, worked at the Nanaimo Pacific Biological Station, taught school in Delta, and has spent many years doing private tutoring and farming. Both have BSc degrees from the University of British Columbia. Both have been involved in historical research, with Harold devoting much time to the Britannia Heritage Shipyard Society and Gulf of Georgia Cannery Society, and Kathy keeping the financial and historical records for the Steveston Historical Society.

The City of Richmond developed a float, a ramp and a dock at London's Landing in 1994 as part of its trail system. (1995)(MY)